SPIRIT
DRIVEN
AUTO SALES

A Sales Guide
With A Higher Purpose

Written By: C.J. Penn

Notes:

2

Dedicated To:

This book is dedicated to the all the salespeople that get their teeth kicked in by rude managers, hostile customers, and unforgiving spouses and still do the right thing when faced with temptation. I admire those resilient enough to get off the canvas, grab a mouthpiece, and stand nose to nose with another sales day.

After finding success, do not step in the snare of coasting because the only way to coast is downhill. Instead, vow never to quit learning and keep ahead of the market. Be humble and recognize learning opportunities and take advantage of them.

Resourcefulness is at your core and it doesn't go unnoticed.

Thank you, my dear reader, for investing in yourself and proving that you're wise enough to fill your head with knowledge, heart with empathy, and future with karma's fruits.

Table *of Contents*

Chapter *Four* – Developing Attitudes

Nothing Negative
Quality V.S. Quantity
Take All Deals
Clean Cars Cost More
Do it Now! Urgency
Unrealistic Customers
Budget Cars

Chapter *Five* – Protecting Fruit

Balanced Lifestyle
Three Keys to Physical Health
Emotional Health
Community Involvement
Work Satisfaction
Spiritual Health
Mentorship
Karma-Based Decisions

Chapter *Six* – Building the Customer Base

Repeat Customers
Referrals
Prospecting
      Expert within the Circle
      Indirect
      Direct

Chapter *Seven* – Harmony

Personality Gifts
Finance Managers
Detailers
Service Writers
Service Techs

Introduction

What makes high performers tick? How do they sell so many vehicles? Do they really do it with half the prospects? Can a brand-new salesperson outperform industry leaders? *The answer is yes*. And it is easier than you think.

My teachings come from a unique view.
- A struggling salesperson within a dealership that had no training program.
- A high producer on a sales team with a stunning training program.
- A trainer that developed others from the ground up.
- A Managing Partner in a franchised dealership.
- A person who developed six managers who went on to run their own dealerships.

Regardless of the hat worn, I carried a salesperson's heart and never forgot their struggles along the way. Most managers have long forgotten the sales floor grind and are out of touch with the front-line soldiers. I never strayed from my core.

Despite losing those six top-level employees, our store flourished through the toughest conditions that the Auto Sales industry has ever endured. Not to be confused with perfection – very much the opposite. Instead, I learned from mistakes that are sure to accompany over 6,000 sales – failed forward – meaning fell down and got up with greater insight and one step closer to the goal.

What happens when we combine things that feed each other? In racing, we combine horsepower and traction, which equals a faster racecar. UFC fighters combine ground game with standup to produce an effective warrior. Husbands and wives combine discipline, nurturing, and biblical teachings to produce balanced children (and 10,000 prayers). Each element strengthens the whole and makes it more effective.

What about high-performing salespeople?

They combine rapport, process, and technique.

We start with these and grow after adopting the right attitudes. These attitudes clean our hearts and let the world see who we are and why they should buy from us – all combining to produce a better salesperson. We follow a Road to the Sale process with every prospect, build rapport along the way, and reveal our Spirit-driven character throughout the journey. This combination produces a salesperson that runs circles around the slick talkers. *I enjoy that the most* – knowing that a Spirit-driven salesperson eats more fruit. Customers see through the shenanigans and gravitate toward people operating with a pure heart.

My goal is complex: Deliver a book that meets a person wherever they are, regardless of skill level.

- A brand-new salesperson perplexed about learning a tough industry.
- An established salesperson interested in getting to the next level.
- A seasoned veteran that yearns for deeper meaning.

Spirit Driven is at the core of this book, meaning our Creators Spirit – God's Spirit lives in those who request it. I've wandered full circle regarding leading a Spirit-Driven life – reckless without it, and ate much good fruit while obeying instruction, which is exactly how this book was born.

"Dear Lord, please help me lead others to you for what they see in me.
In Jesus name we pray – amen. "

Chapter *One*

Rapport

Kayson and Tom start at Barselco Auto the same day. Kayson knows nothing about selling and is intimidated about the unknown. What am I supposed to be doing? Where should my focus be? Doubt is constant. Tom, on the other hand, has worked in the auto industry for years and needs very little help. He hits the ground running and adapts quickly. Kayson's only skill is getting people to like him and his innocence bleeds through on every deal – yet, he excels for weeks. Tom, the experienced salesperson, struggles to sell and grows frustrated. He blames many things: Managers, inventory, and even a bad-luck run of customers. *Hmmm...* How did zero skills outperform an experienced salesperson?

Rapport.

This exact scenario dances throughout many sales floors across the country. Furthermore, it's amazing how quickly Kayson becomes Tom. *Ouch!* Many salespeople start strong and then fall off after 60 days. Some correct themselves, yet others quit. *Huh? Almost everyone falls down? Yup.*

"Why do good recruits slump after two months?" I asked other GMs.

"They just do, get used to it." Was always the same response.

What? Get used to it? *Negative*, I do not comply.

Why waste the energy poured into new recruits? And what about falling in love along the way? *Oh, crap.* That slipped. Yes, guilty as charged. After spending the energy to develop someone, I am committed to provide and shelter through a watchful eye.

Failure... *Cue broken heart.*

With this in mind, I rejected they just do, and paid close attention to new recruits around the 45-day mark. *Ah, HA!* Pegged it. The explanation was rather simple: After learning new skills, recruits neglected building rapport, and when rapport diminished – so did sales.

Kayson sold so many vehicles because getting people to like him was all he knew how to do and he did it well. The customer simply overlooks, or forgives, Kayson for what he doesn't know throughout the sale. With a little help, Kayson outsells half the staff. Customers let him figure it out as he goes. Honest mistakes are not viewed harshly, and things like product knowledge become non-factors as they both figure out the vehicle together.

> ***Rapport*** *is the glue*
> *that holds deals together*

Here lies the problem – eventually Kayson grasps additional skills and learns how to sell on his own, which swells his confidence. He mistakenly assumes his new sales skills outweigh rapport. Kayson doesn't know it, but he's at a crucial crossroads: Turn left into frustrations and the blame game, or turn right onto correction Blvd.

Ok, Chief. Take me to the Rapport Well and show me how to drink.

Rapport is misunderstood, so let's define it. Webster defines rapport as: Harmonious; one accord. Getting customers to like you is a good idea, yet it falls short of True Rapport, likewise with trust. One builds trust, yet again falls short. True Rapport, means the salesperson and customer reached a level of trust, likability, and moving in the same direction.

Salespeople fall into the trust trap every day, working just hard enough to gain trust then pull back assuming it is enough. Unfortunately, they are half-right because that is enough to stand out in a world of lukewarm salespeople. Gaining trust isn't enough to be a high performer; we must get to one accord.

Our creator sums this same line of thought up nicely:

*"So, because you are lukewarm, and neither hot or cold,
I will spit you out of my mouth."*

Revelations 3:16

Translation: Follow God with all your heart and live by faith— or live without it. Either have faith in His ways and trust His will, or don't believe at all.

Oh, OK. Roger that, Captain.

Likewise, salespeople that refuse to move towards being one accord are lukewarm and should be spit out.

Build *True Rapport* in four ways:

- ✓ Common Ground
- ✓ Feeling Understood
- ✓ Teaming Up
- ✓ Control

Common Ground – we gravitate to others who share our same likes and interests. A stranger becomes something more after finding out they share our interests. *Oh,* you're a Denver Broncos fan? You can't wait to see Arturo Gotti go to war in the ring? The sound of a racecar idling makes your heart quiver too? *Well then,* we are ~~sick~~ cut from the same cloth – pull up a chair my friend.

Engage in conversation and hunt for common ground. Things like children, sports, work, and ~~fight~~ club memberships are great places to start. Once finding common ground, keep them talking and find more areas.
Dubbed: *Slowing the customer down.*
A customer's vehicle throws off hints such as, bumper stickers, fishing poles, or a key chain displaying a favorite team. These things are a source to build common ground – not to be confused with chameleon that takes any interests and makes them his or her own.
Ish, ish, ish. PaaaTHUP
<wiping spit from chin>

Insincere flattery is a poison pill that won't be swallowed by anyone. Instead, find connectedness through **actual** common ground.

Silly question, Mate. What happens when there is no bond? *Well,* it's too easy to say no. Without a connection, the relationship stays all business: YOU vs. THEM.
Telling a salesperson no is easy, yet it's quite different telling a friend no (especially bail requests - *errr*). Therefore, become a friend and build the sale from there.

Feeling Understood - Dale Carnegie wrote *How to Win Friends and Influence People* decades ago, yet it still remains the gold standard for interacting with strangers to

14

this day. Folks love to talk about themselves, and the quickest way to make a good first impression might surprise you – *shut up*.

Yup. that's right, SHUT UP and get them talking.

Ask open-ended questions, sit back, and allow customers to talk. These plants good feelings within their heart, and with a little water, they sprout roots. Open-ended questions are ones that cannot be answered with a yes or no

---

Questions such as:

- What line of work are you in?
- What do you enjoy about your job?
- How has your work changed?
- What are your plans after retirement?
- What are your kids up to?
- How did you meet your spouse?
- Is this the first place you have been?
- How is the shopping going so far?

?

They must engage and explain answers, and little by little, the person blossoms.

Care to spark the eyes of a retiree? Just ask what they did before retirement. An ounce of good open-ended questions produces a pound a rapport.

After finding common ground, move on to assessing needs. Resist throwing out product ideas before earning a voice through qualifying questions – *hey*, suggestions are a powerful thing but until you've earned the right to give them, *don't*. Great danger lies in making assumptions. Much fruit comes in the form of slowing down and making sure you are on the correct path. Be thorough and probe every angle to show that the client's needs are more important than your own.

Here are a few ideas:
- What is the vehicle going to be used for? Especially truck buyers.

- Who will be using the vehicle? Don't assume that there is only one user. Strive to understand everyone's needs.

- What kind of vehicle were you looking for when you purchased your current vehicle? Many people settled for something outside their goal and ended up with a vehicle they didn't want.

- How long do you plan to keep your next vehicle?

- How many miles per year do you drive?

Understanding needs is a giant step toward *True Rapport*. One accord means being on the same page and unless we figure out their motives we haven't arrived yet. Gather relevant information and mold a clear picture of needs, once that picture comes into focus *then* make suggestions. Throwing out ideas before understanding needs is the same as a stranger insisting a blind date. Surely, a friend's opinion is worth more. Why? They understand needs and aim to fulfill them – the same principle applies when leading precious customers to their perfect vehicle.

Engaging in conversation and hunting for common ground is the first step to build True Rapport – let us call it the spark of a new relationship. Then we understand needs through specific questions – shall we say that we have reached over and grabbed the hand of our new friend, now it's time to become *one accord.*

Teaming Up – One accord means one agenda, something rare in the sales world. Profit certainly spells T.R.O.U.B.L.E., doesn't it? One side is tickled pink to purchase at thousands below cost and the other side enjoys lobbing fat paychecks to smiling spouses. So how do we make this work? The short answer: Think *long term.* When salespeople protect future business, they are heading the right direction.

Ok, Champ. Grab your One Accord uniform, you're going in.

Customer + Salesperson V.S. Dealership.

Try these great tips.
- Look over the vehicle with customers instead of leaving the inspection up to them.

- Point out scratches and dents rather than popping the hood and walking away.

- Pull dipsticks and explain what to look for: Low oil levels, low coolant levels, mismatched paint, replaced body parts.

Carry this further during the test drive. Ask if the brakes pulsate, brake hard and make sure it doesn't pull to one side, and turn a tight circle with four-wheel drive engaged to verify its working properly (front wheels will hop on dry pavement).

By helping identify these things, or lack of these things, is a great way to have your customers back. And makes a loud statement: We are a team! This behavior builds rapport so strong that by the time they reach the worksheet step it isn't a question *if* they are buying – it is a matter of *how* they will buy.

"What do you think we should offer them?"

What a great indicator that you have done a good job building True Rapport, and you've treated commission as secondary.

Rapport Killers – We talked about gaining traction now let's discuss ways not to bang rapport off the backstretch walls.

Ignoring the Female slaps rapport in the face. Don't jam a foot in your mouth by assuming the male is the decision maker and ignoring the female.
I just love this part – grab a chair.
This is a crucial mistake. First off, *most* of the time, the female *is* the decision maker and excluding her ruins the chance to build rapport with the ~~dominant~~ correct person. So how does one know when to target the female?

That's easy: *EVERY TIME.*

By always assuming that the female is the decision maker you're playing it safe, and if she isn't? She will defer you back to the male *allowing* the attention to shift to him (God doesn't have a sense of humor? *Huh!*). Offended males can send disgruntle letters to 123 God's Divine Plan Blvd. Please refrain from using mismatched color crayons and please have the nearest female proofread before sending.

Cue Ginalicious

Poor Eye Contact – somewhere embedded within us is a little system that registers eye contact as impactful. A casual encounter instantly turns into something significant when eyes meet squarely, whether waiting for a glazed doughnut at my father's favorite bakery, walking through a crowded room, or a redheaded child glaring from a timeout corner (whoa kid, *chill*). Eye contact helps connect at a deeper level. In contrast, poor eye contact makes people wonder: *What are they hiding?* You could be doing everything right, but failure to look up and meet eyes periodically erodes trust. They sense something amiss and look for things to reinforce their screaming gut.

Confession: During my first year, I struggled with healthy eye contact – floating between not giving enough, and going overboard with the dreaded stalker stare (hey, she was enchanting). *Cue practice.*

First, give good eye contact to service people such as gas station attendants and wait staff, and within a few days it rolls into other areas, like holding doors open, or light bumps come with an apology and eye contact. Next, meet strangers in the eye and following it with a hello. *Yup,* simple dimple. Finally, drive home significant sales points with eye contact rather than every little detail. Driving home minor details is like crying wolf, which dilutes key areas. Within a couple weeks, this forms a great habit, one I carry to this very day, and the fruits of countless good first impressions.

In closing, I have yet to work with a high performer that doesn't use eye contact effectively. I challenge you to form this habit and take notice of the things that flicker your way because of it.

Unexplained Idle Time – dealerships are horrible at leaving customers in the dark at points in the sales process. Two specific times: First, waiting for trade appraisals, and secondly, after agreeing on numbers and waiting for finance. Customers get testy during these waiting periods, and we lose rapport if not handled correctly. Waiting is outside the salesperson's control so rather than getting upset – use it to your advantage. Give these statements a whirl.

"When the appraiser takes extra time, it means he's interested in your trade, rather than just tossing numbers out of thin air."

"I've given your information to finance, they will shop around to get the best terms, sometimes it takes a while but it saves you money."

Translation: It's going to be a minute, Bud

Address stalls before they happen, and if primed correctly, customers view the wait time as a money-saving activity. Use this time to review owner's manuals, service walks, or move trade items to the new vehicle.

One more thing: Does a husband remind his wife about childbirth right before kissing her ear? Um, *heeell* no. Likewise, talk about anything BUT the car deal – leave a closed door shut or risk unwinding the deal.

<hiding the wine>

Asking for The Sale Too Early – new salespeople, all too often assume that having enough ~~cojones~~ courage to ask for the sale is a sign of strength... this couldn't be further from the truth. Although, confidence is a good sign, holster that brashness until the time is right.

When is the right time? Great question.

- [ ] During the walk around? Nope, too early.

- [ ] During the test drive? Nada, still too early.

- [x] After returning from the test drive

> ## "Sell product on your feet and hold gross on your seat."

Translation: Refuse discussing numbers while presenting products.

Without all the details to make an educated decision, the answer will be no, and once that flops out, prospects look for things to reinforce that decision. Non-factors are now used to support the refusal. Trial closing is the correct way to ask for the sale, discussed later in the Road to The Sale Chapter.

Unknown Answers – Unfamiliar questions will come up, so don't allow the sale to go sideways by dropping everything to get it answered. Instead, write the question down and agree to come back to it. Most questions are not deal breakers and allowing them to halt the sales process discredits the salesperson and reduces rapport.
Can you keep a secret?
Some customers know more about vehicles then salespeople do, especially truck buyers. Savvy buyers throw questions just to gauge responses. *Will they lie to me?* How a person responds reveals character, doesn't it? Don't assume your value is measured by how much information is known – it's not. Handle questions thoroughly, at the right time, and customers will appreciate your level or control, and trust you with bigger things.

Poor Hygiene – like it or not, people judge others based on appearance. A Spirit-blessed person withholds judgment, but let's face it – others will devalue a person based on wrinkled clothes, bad breath, and unkempt hair. Great skills fail to overshadow poor hygiene.

Why should I allow a person to take care
of my needs if they refuse their own?

Some dealers go overboard requiring suits, ties, and bling (boo!). Dressing to match the core market makes more sense to this fella. Regardless, carry good hygiene to either place.

Iron clothes, trim facial hair, and keep a current haircut. The real stinker sits just under your nose: bad breath. Make a pact with coworkers: if the bad breath fairy squatted in my mouth – please tell me. We make our living talking up close and personal, so why push this topic away over pride? Keep a box of mints nearby and use them often.

Broken Promises – not exactly Rocket Science, yet it rears its ugly head from Poskin, WI to Navarre, FL. Here's the problem: Salespeople make promises that others fulfill.

Anyone feel a headache brewing? I do.

The salesperson promises to fix repairs, dents, dings, tears, cigarette burns, or new tires and then throws that actual work on someone else's lap. What if that lap is full? On vacation? Or ~~weeping~~ sitting in a Tijuana jail cell? Many things thwart promises.

The best defense is rather simple: Don't make promises. Salespeople allow molehills to become mountains and mistakenly assume minor things hinder a sale. Consequently, they promise to take care of every little thing and end up with many hanging issues.

Veterans know better.

Handle these things during negotiation because we're forced to discount anyway. If unavoidable, fill out a 'We-Owe' form to be signed by the salesperson, manager, and customer. Our logic is twofold: Preventing "selective" memory *and* that form triggers a process. Through process, we protect our ~~derriere~~ customer.

One last stop on the Rapport-Building Train before departing.

Controlling Customers – controlling customers is a daunting task because every customer is unique and has a mind of his or her own. Toss in thousands of products– *shake vigorously* – and disaster ensues. Without an organized plan, we feel like a can tied to a dog's tail.

What does this have to do with rapport?

Everything

Effective control ripens confidence. Customers sense this confidence and grant a deeper level of trust.

METAPHOR ALERT:

Brady and Fred start a tour guide business in Maui, Hawaii. Fred plans on learning as he goes and hopes everything turns out well. His first clients arrive and they embark on the lush terrain. Fred is reluctant to do anything except wander aimlessly through the surroundings. In fact, he tails the clients. They walk off path and brush up against poisonous plants, travel down dead ends, and miss breathtaking views. Fred makes light conversation and the clients genuinely like him, yet they feel the tour was a waste of time.

Brady, on the other hand, uses a different approach. Going through the same lush terrain, he *leads* his clients and points out different plants, animals, and landmarks along the way. They find the Seven Pools and stop at stunning

24

waterfalls – things that other vacationers miss. When his clients veer off the path, he carefully convinces them to keep following – pointing out dangers as they go. Brady refers to his map often and makes sure they pass through many important sites. Rather than following the client, Brady leads the way stopping periodically to check in. He fills down time with stories about the area and his favorite parts, which gives his customers a great *experience.*

Who earns greater trust, and why?
Which person is more likely to get referrals?

Brady by far, and the reason is simple: He took control. *But, but, but,* Brady knew all the little details, wasn't that the reason for better results? *Agreed*, but the experience was better because of process (the map). Brady kept on course because he had a predetermined plan and stuck to it. The details mentioned along the way were basics and only took a few minutes to memorize. Fred and Brady both carry likeable personalities, but Brady's confidence and control sets him apart.

Wait for it — unorganized salespeople are just like Fred, hopelessly following the client. Wise salespeople control their customers though a *Road to the Sale* process, or map. Instead of heading off path, they contain customers and enjoy better results.

Ugh. Really? I cannot be me?
I have to follow a boring process?

Check the math on that one bud. It's not about picking one or the other – it's about combining personality and process. Salespeople keep their flavor throughout the Road to the Sale process, yet stay disciplined and move safely through the process – the result is confidence.

In addition, set the tone through light commands. Start early, like when the prospect first enters the store and again when you need them to stay seated.

"Please have seat and I'll be right over."

"Wait here while I pull your vehicle up."

"Wait here in case the bank has any questions."

Light commands work wonders for controlling where your customers are and what they do. As with everything, this takes time to feel natural – but they are an crucial part of controlling your environment.

My sales career drastically changed (literally overnight) after joining a sales team that had absolute faith in the Road to the Sale process, and using it wasn't optional. Life's full of choices: Complete every step or sell for a different team. *Hmmm...*

Until then, my results were barely above average (*gulp*), and one month later, I consistently doubled second place, and never looked back. The Road to the Sale helped me sell more vehicles, hold more profit, and produce happier customers.

Cue splitting clouds.
Still riding the fence?
Let's reflect on an actual deal:

Confession: I'm three shades beyond the biggest goofball you know – *especially* while working deals. I got stuck in the Sense of Humor Line when God installed off buttons – and I thoroughly enjoy earning a hard-fought smile on a gruff old-timer's face.

For example, a retired-aged couple visited our store and the 300-pound husband shook the windows while pounding his chest. His hard-nosed attitude was tough to deal with and he quickly ran over his original salesperson. *Yikes, here we go.*

The original salesperson turned the customer over to me after growing frustrated — most salespeople refuse to deal with rude shenanigans of this nature.

How should I handle Mr. Grumpy?
Hmmm...

Besides bringing them down the Road to the Sale, I might as well have some fun along the way. *Overfloweth thy cup, perhaps?* Let's take a stop or two down smile Blvd, shall we? I sat them down and filled out a needs assessment form and made some light-hearted jokes. No smile from

Mister Grumpy through any of the first steps –
hmmm – better double down on the goofy antics.
Every rapport-building question returned a grunt,
blank stare, and cracking knuckles. *Ouch!*

Accept defeat, or kick it up a notch?
Yup. Insert another quarter.

We landed on a fully loaded Ford
Expedition and moved to the worksheet step. Not
wanting to fail within view of staff, and a good
deal of personal pride, I pushed forward.

Negotiation should be a treat.

Mr. Grumpy made a big mistake: He
brought his sweetheart wife along. She glowed
bright enough to make a chandelier blush. *Oh, oh.*

I brought out two papers: The first
contained starting numbers, which I laid upside
down, and the other was blank. I began my pre-
flop line, but refused to turn the paper over to
display the price. He couldn't wait to brow beat
me. He sat sharpening his arrows and had the bow
pulled back waiting to fire. Again, I refused to
turn the paper over. Instead, I wrote "Grumpy
Grandpa" on the second sheet, and told him that I
was no longer speaking to him – but would
consider speaking to his wife – providing he
smiles, and then, *and only then,* he was allowed to
whisper in his wife's ear. Then, *she* could relay
his messages. A loop of string secured it safely
around ~~The Bear's~~ Grumpy Grandpa's neck.

Finally. Secured. My. Smile.
(Send my snazzy ribbon to Poskin, WI.)

Yes, he still made me work for the sale – and bless her heart – his wife refused to repeat half of the things he whispered in her ear, which did make an easier sale. The sale was rewarding but the real prize wandered in a few months later: *Referrals.*

Grumpy Grandpa sent others our way.

What's the moral of the story? To install a big red nose and oversized shoes before trekking to work? *No.* Trust the Road to the Sale but also bring your flavor along for the ride, this combination sets you apart from others in ways that cannot be measured.

Additional smiles free of charge.

Full Circle – who benefits the most from building rapport? The salesperson grasps an easier sale so it must be them, but is it? Salespeople perfect ways to build rapport, and trick themselves into believing rapport is for their benefit. Although true, a much greater dynamic is at play. As a Managing Partner, I noticed a very odd thing.

Do salespeople care more, or less, about a person they have common ground with? More. *Much more.*

Wouldn't they push to protect that newfound friendship, and ensure their new friend's problems are handled? *Yup*, they fight much harder. True rapport elevates everyone to friends and family status. Therefore, building rapport swings full circle and affects the salesperson as much, or greater than its intended target – building relationships so strong that they fight tooth and nail to take care of issues.

Do you hear that? *Yup.* The repeat-sale fairy is whispering sweet nothings in your buyer's ear long after signing the paperwork.

One more key point before moving on.

Warts and All – buckle up, let's head to Fake Blvd. What do you think when you listen to a friend or family member interact with others completely out of their character? A raspy voiced, chain smoker mimics a dolphin voice while standing in front of their kid's teacher.

Um, yeah – *fake.*

This same stunt happens on the sale floors and it's enough to make customers sick.

Kiss. Of. Death.

Resist perfection. Customers long for real people. Those that show the same face regardless whom they are staring at, and not afraid to let others see them as they really are and dammit, this includes – *gasp* – light swearing. Research confirms that people trust others more if they swear. *Hmmm, interesting.* Swearing is a part of our daily lives and people grant a deeper level of trust to authentic people. Not to be confused with a drunken sailor that just dropped a bottle of Bacardi 151 on their toe – keyword, *light* swearing.

He, who has never been embarrassed, raise that hand nice and high. *Uh, huh.* Just as I thought, no one. Share embarrassing stories – being vulnerable opens the door for others to join you on the ground floor.

Be vulnerable. Be yourself. Be real.

True rapport is the secret to high performers and ironically the very skill that accompanies recruits from day one. Use these tips to gain rapport quickly, and cling to it as a toddler clings to the sides of the pool, even after learning additional skills. If results slip, immediately evaluate whether you're neglecting hunting for common ground and teaming up with your customer. Even if a buyer comes in with a check in hand ready to purchase sight unseen (rolling eyes), a wise salesperson slows down and gets to know him or her before moving forward.

In closing, if God grants you the ability to build deep rapport, and gain the trust of others – in return, He holds us to a higher standard, and our actions should reflect this higher standard. Specifically, have your customers back and work hard to meet their needs. They grant you trust, and you grant them a servant.

"Everyone to whom much is given of him, much will be required."

Luke 12:48

Chapter *Two*

Road to the Sale

"*For we walk by faith, not by sight.*"

2 Cor 5:7

This passage speaks about living one's life confidently trusting in God's promises for the future, even when we cannot see the fullness of the coming glory. In the same way that believers trust what they cannot see, a salesperson works in trust of the Road to the Sale process. The glory of the sale isn't visible in the beginning steps, but faith in the process leads us down the correct path.

Drag thy beast across thy stump; it's time to chop up our main process.

The Road to the Sale greatest benefit isn't selling more vehicles, holding additional gross, or producing happier customers – the *training* benefits outweigh all. As you know, learning the sales industry is a daunting task. Folks choke on the full plate and most new salespeople end up ~~quitting~~ with digestion overloaded. A constant inner voice challenges everything.

Is this the most important thing for me to be doing? Where should I focus? Am I doing this right?

We break down The Road to the Sale into ten bite-sized chunks, chew one step at a time, and use it as a training program. *Silence, Mr. Doubt! BE GONE*. Learn step one, role play until it's natural, and then move on.

Lather rinse repeat.

Ten steps later, we have a solid backbone and advance to other areas. The secret lies in its simplicity. Vehicles are not sold in one clean swoop, instead the goal is to simply reach the next step, and it eventually results in a sale. The best part: If you fail getting to the next step, get help, and then fall back into learn mode. Shadowing quickens the learning curve. Wrapping arms around a sale is overwhelming, but the next step is much easier, so take baby steps to the finish line. Our goal moves from selling the vehicle to obtaining the next step.

Step 1: Meet and Greet – "Hello, my name is Jax. Follow me inside to get started." Then turn and walk away. Pausing and inviting conversation slashes the chance of making it to step two.   This is the *Walk-Away Method* and it works beautifully to get customers inside and under control.

Step 2: Qualified – From here forward anytime the term: needs assessment, qualified, or registered is used, it refers to the same thing – gathering relevant sale information to help customers make educated product selections.

Twofold goal: (A) building rapport through the methods discussed in the last chapter, and (B) get a completely filled out registration form.

Think pendulum.

Swing back and forth between gathering needed information (form), and pausing to build rapport. Feel free to stop, sit back, and ~~hunt for smiles~~ engage in conversation.

"God blessed us with two ears and only one mouth, we should listen twice as much as we talk."
-Mark Twain

All dealers use a variation of the same Needs Assessment form and obtaining the needed information can be done in five minutes with force that would make an interrogator squirm, or gathered slowly to set a healthy tone. Find healthy eye contact, slow your speech, and engage playful energy. *Pa pa pleeese pick option two.*

The Or System. Reader, please step forward and meet your new best friend:

CAR			SUV			TRUCK		
2 DR	4 DR		4 WD	RWD	AWD	RWD		4WD
Stick	Automatic		2 Row		3rd Row	R/C	S/C	C/C
Domestic	Foreign		Domestic		Foreign	Domestic		Foreign
Basic Model	Nicer Model		Basic Model		Nicer Model	Basic Model		Nicer Model
4 cyl	6 cyl	8 cyl	4 cyl	6 cyl	8 cyl	Gas		Diesel
Small	Mid	Large	Small	Mid	Large	Long Box		Short Box
Under how many miles?			Under how many miles?			Small	1/2 Ton	1 Ton
						Under how many miles?		

Using the **OR** system allows us to funnel down, yet leave plenty of wiggle room to fit multiple vehicles. At the date of this publication, used car factories are almost extinct, spreading panic across sale's floors everywhere. Thus, leaving heartbroken salespeople that are no longer able to take used vehicle orders.

Hey, smart Alec. Used Car Factories never existed.

Oh, MY BAD. If we cannot "order" used vehicles, then we'd better use a system that fosters flexibility. Adding options opens more doors.

Never assume your customer isn't flexible.

Avoid painting yourself into a comer with questions like, "What color would you like?" This is like setting a baseball atop an 8ft tee at a peewee game, except there will be no giggles while swinging your sales bat at a hard to reach car. A much better approach: "What colors are out of the question?"

Prospects fall in line throughout this dance, which allows multiple choices. *Ok, Boss*. Whaddabout specific buyers? Surely, some customers demand certain vehicles, right? *Rare, but true*. Sway fussy buyers by asking if it's more important to get exactly what they want or a good deal? Anyone smell the indirect message: Are you willing to pay more for exactly what you want? If yes, well at least there is incentive to wrestle up a ladder to reach the sale.

New Car Buyers, on the other hand, have every justification to get exactly what they want; in fact, they can order vehicles directly from the factory with every wish granted, hence joking about the used car factory.

Ordering used vehicles is unrealistic, and most customers' settle for a vehicle close to their goals so don't let exceptions push you to mishandle the masses. Assume everyone is flexible, and when you run into someone who isn't – then make sure the juice is worth the squeeze.

Up To-But Not More Than method works to get a payment range, rather than a hard number. Here's how it would look:

Sales: What is your desired payment?
Buyer: $250
Sales: Up to how much?
Buyer: $300
Sales: But not more than how much?
Buyer: Not more than $350.

This method produces a wider payment range, which opens more doors. A wider payment range increases the chance of landing on a vehicle. If we accept the starting payment of $250/mo. we've severely limited our options. The additional $150/mo. bump opens an $8,000-dollar window. *Not* to be confused with selling a $250/mo. vehicle for $350/mo. We show the lowest, cheapest, vehicle first and simply trying to open more doors if the customer rejects the first selection. Most customers spit out a payment goal of $250/mo. yet are willing to pay more for the right vehicle.

Identify this range early.

Payment Buyers don't mind disclosing payment goals but Cash Buyers hold these cards close to their chest (shocker). It makes sense, doesn't it? Why tell a commission-based salesperson how much cash you are willing to part with? Even so, pry out a ballpark number to get a starting point.

Address this in two ways: guess a price range (based off the vehicle desired info), or a throw out an obscene number and let the customer correct you.

Sales: What price range would you like to stick to?
Buyer: It doesn't matter.
Sales: I need a place to start. What did you have in mind?
Buyer: It really doesn't matter. What do you have?
Sales: I'll try and keep you under fifty thousand dollars, does that work for you?
Buyer: Keep me under twenty-two thousand dollars.

I have yet to meet a customer that didn't redirect from fifty thousand dollars. You can use the **Up To but Not More Than** method here as well, but tread *veeerrry* lightly. Again, this tactic isn't about making more money – it's about having a starting point and a wider range of vehicles to show. We work within a short window and don't want to squander time.

If financing, always get credit information. Some dealerships don't gather credit information until after landing on a vehicle; this mistake crashes many deals. What happens when a customer falls in love with a vehicle and then cannot get approved? They are disappointed – so much so, that they leave rather than trying to get approved on something else.

They eventually end up buying,
just not from you. *Gulp*.

Credit info helps land on vehicles that match payment goals, down payment goals, and lender guidelines. Address these items before Cupid flings his arrow, not after.

What happens if you spend four hours with a customer that needs a cosigner, and they don't have one? The salesperson *and* customer are deflated – by no means am I implying that we don't work with low credit customers, treat everyone with respect, but knowing these things early helps address the situation effectively. We can be just as effective in 20 minutes as in two hours. Respect everyone's time and energy by collecting enough credit information to run a credit bureau and then select cars that match score-driven guidelines.

Ok, Chief. What if they refuse to shell out their private, personal, and coveted credit information?

If the customer refuses to provide a SSN number and DOB, use this system: "On a scale of 1 to 10, where do you rate your credit?" Instead of writing his or her SSN number down, write down the number given. Any answer less than a 10 is followed with, "What would drop it to that number?" Hopefully, this draws out a bankruptcy or other fruitful details. The 1-10 method isn't the best for matching customers to vehicles, but it's better than nothing. This method is the exception, not the rule.

Um, well, I am still uncomfortable asking for credit information. What if I offend them?

Gathering credit information early is the mark of a professional. When new, this creates anxiety – we simply haven't been involved with credit related issues before and because this is a sensitive area, we walk on eggshells. The auto industry isn't the only one that understands this process. Savvy real estate agents wisely do the same. They refrain from showing houses until they know a buyer's credit, income, and payment goals.
     Begin with the end in mind.

Showing a $200,000-dollar home to a buyer that cannot handle a payment over $500/mo. is a disaster begging to reveal itself – we operate the same way. *Serious* buyers don't get offended about providing credit information.

Be Complete! – What happens when parents sit down and help kids with schoolwork and they don't have complete information? *No*, drop the switch, ya jerk. Whether it is barely legible, half-missing, or half-hearted, helping becomes much harder, if not impossible. Managers are like parents that help salespeople do homework. *Oh*, OK. In contrast to little Johnny's parents who love him enough to go the extra mile – managers skip sloppy deals and grab one they can be productive on (like you didn't see that coming).

Combat this by filling out every line and slowing down enough to make sure others can read ~~our~~ your chicken scratching. I'm an expert in the appalling handwriting

department. My penmanship was in the top of my class –
for exactly one year – *kindergarten*. In the following years,
not so much. Seeing my deals waiting an extra hour or two
steadied my hand a bit, and when things came full circle and
I became the squinter, I completely understood why it is so
important to get things right the first time.

Efficiency.

Managers must allocate their time to be effective and
– *big surprise* – breaking handwriting codes is the opposite
of productivity.

Managers want enough information on the needs
assessment form to pick out a vehicle without asking the
salesperson a single question – not that they won't, but it
attests as to the level of completeness required. Ideally,
while a salesperson works new clients, an aggressive
manager grabs a stack of needs assessment forms and works
Unsold Prospects. A complete form means getting more
bang for your buck. The initial effort is amplified through
others hands.

All that without using the F word one time.
Fired. Silly...

Many crucial things happen during the needs
assessment, easily making it the most important step in the
Road to the Sale. First, we take control by sitting customers
down and obtaining their full attention. Second, we build
result-producing rapport. Third, thoroughness helps make
customers feel understood – softening hearts in the process.
Fourth, the vehicle desired section, we use "or" questions,
which expands the needle in the haystack to many other
choices. Fifth, we get valuable payment and price goals to
work with, followed by actual credit data to make fact-based

decisions. Finally, we produced a nice clean compact form for future use.

Mmmm. Mm. Mmmm.
Check the oven, our sale smells awfully good.

Practice registrations through role-play – grab a handful of blank registrations and register co-workers, service customers, friends, and family (the cute face licker in aisle five). Repetition creates confidence, so role-play thirty plus times before running live.

Which reminds me of a story:

Casey, my brother, spent the majority of his work life building trusses for a truss factory. During the winter months, he wanted to sell cars.
Cue shivers.
What if he cannot handle this line of work? I nervously accepted. We trained registrations first, and after some role-play, I pointed him to the service waiting area. He practiced registrations on people waiting for oil changes.

What harm could he do there?
They were just waiting for service.

Within three weeks, he sold 16 vehicles – and he never spoke to one person actually looking to buy a car. This is a perfect example of what happens when we lead people down the Road to the Sale. Casey simply gathered information of a hypothetical car deal and then showed vehicles that fit that criteria. Granted, he needed a little help when it came to worksheets but help was available and he learned the balance of his sales skills on the fly.

    Excellent, pass the popcorn.

Step 3: Touch the Desk – dealership dynamics fork right here. Some stores require managers to select vehicles whereas other stores burden the salesperson. New salespeople benefit greatly from the first method, which is my preferred approach as well (regardless of the salesperson's experience). Yet, a large percentage of readers are required to figure this out on their own so let's review the thought process for landing customers on vehicles.

    Always start with the cheapest vehicle that meets their needs. Hey there, do ya see that closet over there? Toss your opinions in there for a minute. *Thank you.* Many people think a fully loaded vehicle means power locks and windows, yet others wouldn't be caught dead in a vehicle without leather, navigation, rims, and a personal masseuse. *Your* opinion might not match *their* opinion, so don't prejudge units – and surely don't reject vehicles *for* customers.

Salespeople aren't decision makers,
they're presenters,
so present options and get feedback.
(arched eyebrow)

Based off the registration form, select three units in a good, better. best mindset and show the good one first. If rejected, move to the better one and if rejected again, go to the best – another rejection, means walking the lot and doing our best to land on a vehicle closest to their goals.

An important dynamic happens when a prospect rejects a vehicle:

Maybe I'll have to be flexible to get what I want.

It also satisfies the urge to look around. Interesting enough, it's amazing how many times the first or second vehicle works. Do not start with the best because it's going to be on the top-end of the goal range. What happens if financing pushes the payment too high? *Cue foot stomps.* What if it's snubbed? Where do you go? *Cue head scratching.* Showing the lower quality vehicle first improves our chances of landing the customer.

Payment buyers – how does one select vehicles if the payments are not known? Like managers – they guess, albeit an *educated* guess. Assume that for every $1,000 dollars financed results in a $20-$30 in payment: $10,000 would be $200 to $300/mo.
(10,000/1000=10 and 10x20=200, 10x30=300).

What about letting customers pick out their vehicles?

BEWARE: Customers will select a $350/mo. vehicle and want it for $200 per month and it's not entirely their fault either; advertising sets this ball in motion. Consequently, don't hold it against people that buy into dealership's absurd claims. By the time you pry their hands off a $350/mo. vehicle, much of the sand in the hourglass has vanished. Avoid squandering time by getting prospects on the Road to the Sale and select vehicles that work for everyone.

Step 4: Pull up the Vehicle – POP QUIZ: What is the risk of walking customers out to the lot to check out the selected vehicle? *Hmmm*. Well, what if they wanna lick a different vehicle's windows? One that doesn't match their goals. *Sure*, the cupid's arrow will find its mark but what happens when that cupid isn't crafty enough to get them to swallow higher payments? NO-SALE.

Pull vehicles up instead.

This eliminates the risk of wandering over to vehicles out of their price range. Remember Brady, the tour guide? Through control, we lead away from potential problems.

Brake rotors rust when they aren't used, especially in high humidity. This occurs because the brake pads clamp down on the rotors to stop the vehicle, which exposes bare metal – and bare metal develops surface rust quickly. No need for alarm. When a vehicle is driven daily, this little rust burns off, but unused vehicles causes buildup, which causes squeaky brakes.

> *Squeaky brakes cause squeaky customers.*
> *Squeaky customers grind sales to a halt.*
> *Halted sales lead to reviewing help wanted ads.*

Combat this by bringing the vehicle up to 10-15 mph and brake hard, thus reducing squeaky ~~customers~~ brakes everywhere. In addition, park in an area where the customer doesn't have to use reverse, it's awkward operating unfamiliar vehicles – especially backing up, so help your customer out.

44

Before exiting, push the driver's seat back and tilt the steering wheel up. This forces the customer to personalize it and clears room for larger drivers. Pop the hood, trunk, and open all the doors before heading back inside to grab your customer.

Step 5: Walk-Around – time to present our product (quick, suck in your gut). Time to give your vehicle the proper attention it deserves. Anxiety buildup releases right here. Car shopping excites customers and they cannot wait to climb behind the wheel (saving terrible salespeople everywhere).

Pump the brakes champ.

A danger lurks, *pushing unwanted vehicles*. We intentionally show the cheapest vehicle first — knowing it might be *too* cheap. Many people are too nice to stop an excited salesperson from going forward. Why would they? You've spent much time building rapport and good energy exist between you, so there's a good chance they'll allow you to show a car they don't like. Combat this by stopping and gauging their first reaction. Signs of discomfort mean switching to your next vehicle – **don't move forward**. Switch units.

Doing a Walk-Around intimidates salespeople. What if they ask a question I don't know? Will I blow the sale? An organized plan ripens confidence but these worries are a waste of time because most competitors don't even do a walk-around. *Almost anything is better than doing nothing.*

In the skills section, we cover a basic, midlevel, and advanced walk-around. Regardless of your product-knowledge, we'll have you up and running.

Step 6: Test Drive – assuming the customer didn't ~~slap~~ reject you during the walk around its time for a test drive. The last step granted your windbags a bright spotlight, so pull the plug. *Yup*, zip it during the first half of the test drive. Driving unfamiliar vehicles can be nerve-racking and a yapping salesperson is ~~a fool~~ frustrating, so ride in silence – for the first half anyway.

After the customer settles in, sell the dealership. First, you sold yourself through a rapport-building registration, and then sold the vehicle during the walk-around – now it is time to sell the dealership. Talk about warranties, return policies, exchange policies, years in business, and why you like working there – these things reinforce that the dealership is a good place to do business. Speak from thy heart. Pick a tough situation and tell how your manager handled it, or how you expect your mother to be treated if she had problems.

Woe to the key tosser, he or she who perches near their desk instead of the passenger seat. How are buying signs identified from inside the building? What about a funny noise, is it brake dust or something serious? The test drive is half inspection and half comfort. Teaming up, means we help inspect the vehicle, which is impossible from inside the building. What about gauging reactions? Rather difficult to catch buying signs from a cozy swivel chair, isn't it? This ~~laziness~~ misstep hurts gross and costs sales by not reading if you are on the right vehicle and needing to switch. High producers determine whether to overcome issues, or ditch plans – this data comes through driver feedback.

46

Step 7: Trial Close – means asking for the sale assuming the terms are agreeable, *without* exact numbers.

?

Is there anything other than price,
that would stop you from buying
this vehicle, right now?"

?

We anxiously want to get to the worksheet step, but have to ensure that we've landed on the right vehicle first. This prevents non-price issues from surfacing during negotiation. Handle issues *before* negotiation. If an issue has already came up such as, "I would never buy a vehicle with Firestone tires." or "The air conditioning isn't working." or the dreaded "You have to marry my daughter first." We can still trial close.

"Is there anything other than the tires, price, or your daughter's hand that would stop you from buy this vehicle, right now?"

The worksheet step launches many people into action and they don't need practice doing appraisals, worksheets, or attempting to close a deal that should have never been written up – prevent an egg-drenched face by trial closing.

Common responses:

- ❖ "It would have to be a good deal." Even though this is a good sign, it's not a commitment. Follow, "So if it's a good deal, you would purchase this vehicle, right now?"

- ❖ "I need to talk to my spouse first." In that case, take a road trip, or invite him or her to the store. Half of the time it's a ploy. Ask if they need to approve the vehicle, or the funds.

Approve funds over the phone.
Breaker, breaker, do you read?

Guys and gals with cold feet, please step forward. You know who you are... Afraid to ruin the sale?
Yup, I get it.
But consider this: How much has already happened? You spent 15-20 minutes building rapport, figured out needs, diligently matched price/payment goals, pulled credit to match lender guidelines, did a good walk around, test drove, *and yes*, agreed to raise freckled-face munchkins.

You earned the right to ask for the sale.

At this point, not having the decision makers present is the only thing that should stall the sale. Be resourceful and get them involved before moving forward, *before* reviewing numbers. Negotiations are cleaner when tackling price or payment only – exclude other factors through trial closing.

Step 8: Worksheet – the worksheet step reviews all the details that go into a car deal: Price, trade value, payments, and term. Some worksheets draw offers, and others pick a payment based on rate and term. Each dealership personalizes worksheets and desk managers are ~~dinks~~ fussy about how they are presented. Therefore, get clear expectations from your manager.

Switch to serious mode and present worksheets with very little emotion. When finished, sit back and ask the customer which option they prefer. *Yes, I get it.* A bit boring. As a profession clown (10,000 hours logged), I *haaaate* tucking that part away, but we must communicate cleanly and ensure everyone is on the same page regarding numbers.

Throw the emotion machine back in gear when drawing offers or using closing tactics. Our goal here is no different from the other steps – we need a commitment in order to get to the next step: Finance.

After getting commitments, countless salespeople make a bonehead mistake – very much reminds me of a pro football player who has a long hard-fought kickoff return and starts his victory dance at the 10-yard line, only to fumble. *Charming.* Watching a fumble scramble is much more amusing than scrambling to hold a sale together.

Sit with closed customers until finance signs them out.

Cue temptation.
Almost anything feels more productive than waiting for finance – but why not hold the ball until crossing the finish line? Cell phones are the biggest reasons for fumbles in today's showrooms. Customers call friends, call family,

check the internet for other vehicles, or a personal favorite: *Calling their kids.* Many deals fall apart because kids want larger inheritance checks than protecting Mom and Dad from a foolish decision. Watching an elderly person limp their busted trade onto winter roads never sat well.

<shudder>

Be Productive

- Move trade items to the new vehicle.
- Review the owner's manual.
- Review scheduled maintenance.
- Complete Service Walks.
- Reviewing vehicle options.

- Match radio presets with the trade presets. Bob Marley, let your spirit step forward.

- Calling Parent Protective Services and turning their ~~brats~~ kids in.

The sale represents a lot of hard work, by many team members, so don't drop the ball by assuming there are more important things to do.

Step 9: Finance – Congrats… now it's time to lay your egg in another's hand. Say a little prayer and get everything the Finance Manager needs to complete the deal. Things like copy of driver's license, insurance cards, credit apps, paystubs, worksheet. etc. Finance Managers hate hunting down information, in fact – most will not.

Did you hear that? Yup, just as I thought.

The ~~snobby~~ Finance Manager just slid a file to the bottom of the pile. That missing insurance card just cost your crew an extra 45 minutes (*shhh,* unofficially of course). Don't shoot the messenger, kid. Just relaying an observation made over 50 plus dealerships (events, not job-hopping), different faces all wearing the same attitude.

The waiting period drives people nuts. *Hurry up and finish already!* Time slows down to a crawl. Don't waste this opportunity.

Perhaps a little ~~metaphor~~ story explains this better:

Jason and Lisa meet online and connect quickly.   While dating, Jason is a perfect gentleman. He opens doors, listens politely, and spends much time getting to know her. If she needs a hand with anything, he's on call and loves helping. Even things he hates, like painting, Jason brushes with a smile.

Things escalate and they marry but before the wedding is even paid for Jason changes his tune and runs cold. Dinner conversations are reduced to grunts and he barely acknowledges her in passing. Projects wither away and he complains about everything.
Sheesh, Jason. *WTH*?

How does Lisa feel?
As if Jason ~~is a dink~~ never cared at all.

Jason = salesperson. *Ouch!*

A friendly salesperson snuggles just long enough to get a signature and then runs cold. Whether it's said or not, customers think: *it was all an act.* Customers know that after they commit the pursuit is over.

Sound familiar?

Every action after that coveted signature is done with a pure heart. So reach over, grab their hand, and pull them back to the vehicle. Show every little feature, do it whole-heartedly, do it with bright eyes, and do it with every customer. These feelings stand long after the negotiation melts away.

Spirit-driven salespeople separate themselves in many areas but none greater than how they treat customers after the sale.

Step 10: Delivery – Thou shall not deliver dirty, foul, or offensive vehicles. Engage courtesy wash, vacuum, and install dealer emblem. Folks *lurve* showing off new vehicles and since your name is stuck to the back, perhaps we should produce a proud one.

Install a dealer key chain and put the Service Writers business card in the owner's manual along with your own.

Customer and Vehicle, we now pronounce you husband and wife. Just check her title; she now carries his or her last name.

You may now kiss your ~~salesperson~~ bride.

Running the Ditch – anytime a salesperson veers off The Road to the Sale, we deem this running the ditch.

Bad bad baaaad.

Skipping steps or showing vehicles before assessing needs is a major red flag. Both indicate low faith in the process *and* the mark of a struggling salesperson. Not sure about you, but I've yet to meet a ditch that didn't offer more dangers then I'm willing to risk. The same dangers accompany customers bouncing outside the Road to the Sale.

Showing a vehicle before assessing needs is especially frustrating. <narrowed eyes> While we're at it, why not rush our daughters off with strange men? *Oh, wait.* Bad things happen when things are rushed? *Um, yeah. Cue commonsense.* Evaluate needs *theeen* show vehicles.

Showing vehicles that are double or triple above their payment goals strikes me as odd? *Gosh.* I wonder how this movie ends? *Pffft!* Lost sale. Or showing vehicles with 150k miles when it's the same payment for one with 50k miles (shorter term on high mileage vehicles).

Think unorganized tour guide. Sounds a bit like brushing against poisonous plants.

Falling in love with unaffordable vehicles...

Bad customer experience...

Unemployment line...

Rules Schmules, who doesn't just *looove* filling out job applications?

Negotiating price before test drives also scrunches my eyebrows together. What good is bickering about price if the vehicle doesn't pass the sniff test? Why engage in a high-conflict-potential negotiation if they don't know if the vehicle is right for them?

Wasted time. Wasted energy. Wasted opportunity.

Sometimes running the ditch is necessary. If customers refuse to play our game, we'll play theirs, either way — *we're playing ball.* In those cases, running the ditch is the exception – not the rule. Even then, do your best to get them back on the Road to the Sale – before the test drive at the very latest. Even the toughest customer expects to give up most of the information on the needs assessment form before driving a dealer vehicle, which gives enough time to back up and get on The Road to the Sale.

In closing, no one digests the Road to the Sale in one sitting. Instead, use each step as a personal training guide – and remember, anytime you fail getting to the next step simply get help. A manager's help is free, but another salesperson's help might cost half a deal. Which is greater – all of nothing or half of something?
Life's full of choices, mate. Pick one.

Master each step and add your personal selling flavor along the way and a six-figure income is well within reach. And more importantly, you'll have a blast in the process.
Amen.

Prediction: Combining chapter one with chapter two produces a sales horse that trots into the top 10% of producers. Follow me to reach the top 5%.

Chapter *Three*

Basic Skills

If I had eight hours to chop down a tree,
I'd spend six hours sharpening the axe.
- Abe Lincoln

Lace up those shin-high boots, chuck a flannel shirt on, and snatch that dull axe it's time to sharpen it.

Objection Handling Skills

Objections are those pesky little darts customers love throwing at our balloons. Some directly, and others lurk for an unguarded salesperson. Most are as harmless as a goldfish fart, while others threaten to sink the ship. *Phew!*

When new, objections bring panic but with a little practice, they lose their teeth. Our goal is to effectively overcome objections and prevent losing momentum by darting off sideways. Things surface during the Road to the Sale and threaten to run us in the ditch. To stay on path, we must learn how to handle objections.

?

Common Objections

That price is too high!

What is my trade worth?

What is my interest rate?

I need to talk to my ~~boss~~ spouse.

I only have five minutes.

?

A system handles these objections, and any others thrown your way.

ABQ System: <u>A</u>cknowledge. <u>B</u>ridge. <u>Q</u>uestion.

Acknowledge the question, bridge it with a bridge phrase, and regain control by asking a question.

"The price is too high." The shopper says while looking at the window sticker.
"Price is important to everyone (acknowledged the question), and I wouldn't expect you to pay more than its worth (bridge phrase), I'm more concerned if there's enough room for your family, does this vehicle have enough seats?" (Ask a question to regain control).

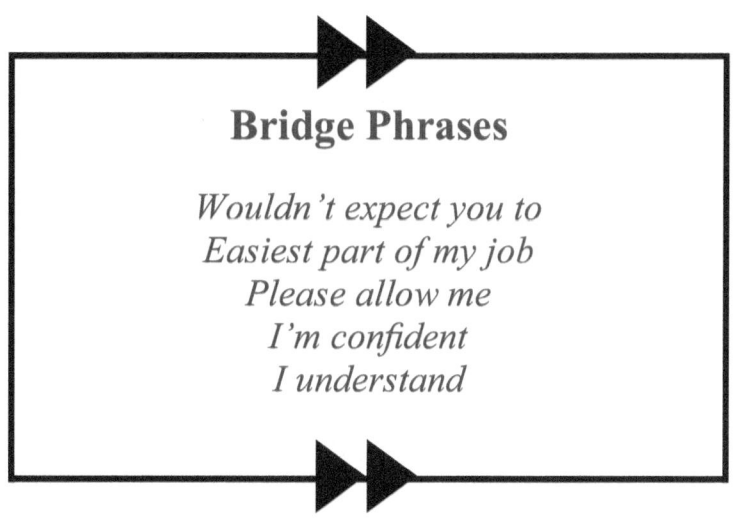

Bridge Phrases

Wouldn't expect you to
Easiest part of my job
Please allow me
I'm confident
I understand

Let's connect these bridge phrases with each objection.

The price is too high!
- ✓ I wouldn't expect you to pay more than its worth...
- ✓ Price is the easiest part of my job...
- ✓ Please allow me to work on that price, but first...
- ✓ I'm confident that I can get that price down...
- ✓ I understand that price is important, let's make sure this vehicle works...

What is my trade worth?
- ✓ I wouldn't expect you to purchase if you didn't get enough for your trade...
- ✓ Trade value is the easiest part of my job...
- ✓ Please allow me to work on the trade amount, but first...
- ✓ I'm confident that I can get you a fair deal for your trade...
- ✓ I understand that trade value is important, let's make sure this vehicle works...

What is my interest rate?
- ✓ I wouldn't expect you to accept an interest rate you didn't qualify for...
- ✓ Interest rate is the easiest part of my job; we have a great finance dept....
- ✓ There are two parts to selling cars, please allow me to work on the first part and finance does the second part.
- ✓ I'm confident that we can get the best rates available...
- ✓ I understand that interest rate is important, it's important to everyone, but let's make sure this vehicle works...

I need to talk to my spouse.
- ✓ I wouldn't expect you to make decisions without including them, but first let's get more details together.
- ✓ Spouses are the easiest part of my job, first let's make sure we have something to discuss with them...
- ✓ Please allow me show you the vehicle so we have some details to go over with your spouse...
- ✓ I'm confident that your spouse will be on board; let's review some things before making that step...

✓ I understand that your spouse is important, let's make sure this vehicle works for them to...

I only have five minutes.
✓ I wouldn't expect you to drop everything if l couldn't find a nice vehicle; give me a chance to help you out...
✓ Valuing your time is the easiest part of my job, give me a bigger window to prove you came to the right place.
✓ Please allow me to show you some great vehicles before you leave. Hopefully, I'll earn a bigger window.
✓ I'm confident that I can make it worth your while to give me a few extra minutes of your time.
✓ I understand that your time is important, but I need a little more than five minutes.

Remove these phrases from the stale canned-phrase's bucket through role-play. Eventually, they are no longer canned and part of your everyday vocabulary. Quicken training by making a deal with coworkers – every time you pass each other throw an objection and handle it on the fly. Within a couple of weeks, you'll have mastered the ABQ method.

If only spouses were handled with such ease.
"I'm sick of your race car."
"I understand, racing isn't important to everyone, but I'm confident that once you see our bank account, you'll have a completely different attitude. Did you want a shoulder rub before or after your bath?" Insert sarcasm and helmet.
*How are all these damn hammer marks
getting on the deck lid? Hmmm...*

Prediction: Once these bridge phrases become second nature, you will pick up extra sales because of other salespeople refusing to work with customers they cannot control. It's fruitful to be known as a person who doesn't get rattled – tough customers will find their way to your desk and these techniques will defuse them quickly and lead to baskets full of fruit.

Apples, bananas, and racing fuel – oooh my.

Follow up Skills

There are two types of follow up: Unsold and sold owner. Unsold follow up are prospects that didn't result in a sale, whereas sold owner follow up refers to people who proudly pedal our vehicles around town. The ability to perform each greatly determines your level of success, because even the most talented salespeople cannot function on daily traffic alone. We address unsold follow up here, and tackle sold owner follow in the Building Customer Base Chapter.

*"Whoever works his land
will have plenty of bread."*
Proverbs 12:11

This verse weaves two unrelated things together, which delivers a universal message. Bread doesn't grow in the ground, yet one works the land to have it.

Translation*: Work your particular field to eat.*

Junkyards work their land by organizing parts, wait staff work their land by being attentive to patron's needs, real estate agents work their land through frequently contacting listings, and salespeople work their land through follow up. Consider this:

METAPHOR ALERT.

Jason has never farmed before but is excited about tending crops. Some grow quickly, and others don't – not knowing which seeds are which he grows frustrated. Sometimes he waters twice a day, yet other times he skips three or four days in a row. Not seeing immediate results, he quits watering altogether.

Cue head scratching and dirt swatting.

Tony, on the other hand, plants so many crops that he cannot begin to manage them all. His crops grow and ripen, but he's off planting more seeds. Tony notices crops missing but isn't concerned. While he's off planting more seeds, harvesters walk off with his ripe crops. Eventually the farm owner sits him down and takes away all his seeds.

Cue breakup music.

Farmhands = salespeople

Salespeople get frustrated with prospects that don't immediately respond to contact (water). Likewise, with the second farmhand that plants seed and doesn't come back to them. Neglecting unsold prospects eventually triggers a manager to remove that salesperson's ability to sell. This is a common issue with aggressive new hires. They skip from prospect to prospect searching for easy sales – failing to realize that every customer will mask their motives the same way.

"They were just looking."

This is muttered by every customer from here to the unemployment line, which is exactly your future if you buy that crap. Struggling salespeople all share this trait and it fails to hold water through a simple method: Stats. 80% of walk-in prospects purchase within 72 hours after they step onto a dealership lot. ***This is why dealerships hound customers***, because they know that someone else will harvests untended crops.

Veterans quickly convert "I'm just looking." to qualifying. They peel off layers and draw out needed information. Even so, they won't sell everyone – thus, creating a need to tend their field through unsold follow-up.

Let's take a second to understand what happens behind the scenes with walk-in and e-lead sources.

Walk-Ins – already decided to purchase long before setting foot on the lot – it's just a matter of *which one*. Thoughts of replacing Old Betsy invaded Ryan and Claudia's suppertime conversations long before hitting the lot and very likely discussed a budget as well. Even if they don't agree on all the details, they discussed what they don't want.

This scene replays across many tables throughout the country. The commitment has already been made before husband or wife *ever step foot outside the home.* Slip this into the memory bank and pull it out whenever we hear: "We are just looking." Make no mistake, they intend to purchase and eight out of every ten prospects run into a salesperson that ignores, "just looking", and ~~embarrasses you~~ harvests the sale.

E-Leads – Internet Buyers are different; the round table discussion hasn't happened yet and either spouse may not be aware the other is ~~sneaking around~~ looking. We still pursue these prospects, but not with the same urgency that walk-in prospects warrant.

Dealer websites are masters at capturing data so if a prospect has bounced around the web, he or she is tangled in many follow up systems, thus creating a highly competitive race to sell.
<releasing the hounds>

Build a presence along their path so when they are ready, you're the first to know.
Mr. Rapport Producer, please step forward.

Two Set Times – should be set aside for doing follow up: Right away in the morning and again right before going home. This forms routines. *And no*, these aren't the only times to water crops – during down time too, which is anytime you're not actively working with customers or preparing for appointments.

Sit within view of the lot so you're not missing fresh opportunities.

Great! Put me in coach but how is follow-up done?

First, let us assume your dealership hasn't joined that fussy thing called the internet and use a full-blown CRM system. In that case, CRM will be a daily way of life. If you don't have a CRM, here are zero-cost methods for watering crops.

Folder Method – save needs assessment forms and comb through them throughout the day. Contact the ones who haven't purchased elsewhere or instructed you to jump off Poskin's Feed Mill. After printing a credit bureau, staple it to the registration form. Having this information in one place makes follow up a breeze. Although over time this folder will bulge at the seams and become cumbersome – but it is still better than doing nothing. Label folders as such.

1. Working Leads
2. Hot Leads
3. Budget Leads
4. Specialty Vehicles
5. Sold
6. Dead (Bought Elsewhere or requested no contact)

Woe to him or her that waits longer than a few days between contact. Work on your hot leads first and contact your working leads according to whatever is holding those deals up, such as waiting for a settlement or spouse approval.

Crops + Water + Harvester = Eat.
Leads + Contact + Salesperson = Sales.

Log Ledger Method – is a simple line-by-line ledger in which we add every deal to a new line. Highlight SALES green, and highlight DEAD DEALS red. Dead deals are prospects that purchased elsewhere or are no longer in the market. This system is effective because of its simplicity. It only takes a minute (literally) to input new prospects, and updating it only takes the swipe of a highlighter. Set the ledger near your work area and contact any prospect that isn't marked in red or green. Contact every working lead, every day.

CRM Method – This stands for Customer Relationship Management, and is the gold standard for follow up. In short, a computer program uses preset triggers that handle sold and unsold follow up. Salespeople enter clients into the CRM and the system takes prospects through a preset process.

Many vendors offer CRM services, and they all look different – but nearly all work the exact same way.

Think internet browsers.

Aren't they all the same? Sure, they all look a little different, but have the same functions: Browsing, favorites, history, ~~viruses~~ and toolbars. Everyone brags about being the best but is really just a preference decision. CRM's companies tout the same attitude but their product functions identical. They all send emails (automatic and user), use reminders, have a note section, print needed forms, collect client data (name. contact info. units purchased, service completed, etc).

Use these tips across all platforms.

Garbage in = Garbage out – a wise man once told me: "If you're going to take time to do something, take extra time and *do it right*." A big thank you to my Grandfather for that wisdom – I obeyed often. Doing CRM right means loading valid information, every time. The system has required fields, meaning you cannot get past a screen without putting data in the box. What if the info isn't known? Fight the urge to enter gibberish, take a couple extra seconds and input valid data.

This information creates important reports and forms. For example, advertising reports detail how prospects enter the dealership, which enables decision makers to make adjustments, *fact-based* adjustments. This helps increase traffic, so valid information helps load your own plate. In addition, automated follow up needs valid data to run, without accurate data the system is unable to contact clients and diminishes the value of the system.

Client Notes – all CRM's have a Client Notes section, which personalizes each client entry and provides a reference to draw from when reviewing deals. Use the notes section as a snapshot and you will easily have relevant information at your fingertips, rather than trying to comb through the entire file.

Use the 1-2-3-4-5 format when adding first notes.

1. Vehicle Desired
2. Payment or Price Goal
3. Cash Down
4. Credit Score
5. City

Example:
1. Explorer – AWD – Leather – V6 – No White - Under 30k miles
2. $350
3. $1,000
4. 633 Score
5. Chetek, WI

Daily Task Sheet – All CRM systems require users to complete daily tasks, and a busy salesperson could easily ~~rear-naked choke the computer~~ become overwhelmed trying to do everything required. Sitting down at a computer, signing in, updating the system, and making fresh notes all takes time. Trying to balance tasks with hawking the lot is frustrating.

Combat this by printing a Daily Tasks Report in the morning and working on it throughout the day, and then update the system before going home. Logging in once, and updating once, keeps the workload light. This gives the best of both worlds: Maximizing the CRM system and grabbing fresh leads throughout the day.

Sending Letters – every day the CRM completes a daily run, which sends out emails and prints letters based off a date-triggered process. For example, the system generates a letter thanking new clients for coming in and then fires off an email. These letters appear as if the salesperson prepared them, but like anything computer generated, have the same feel as a robot reading a bedtime story. *Wa waa waaaa.* Avoid colorless communication by writing a personal message on anything sent out. For example, if my customer was a Cleveland Browns fan and they happen to win their first (and only) game of the season, I would write:

Hey Jim, why burn up your one wish on the Browns? I don't care what the experts say, the Browns could beat most of the college Football teams!

In addition, purchase refrigerator magnets that peel off on one side enabling a business card to be stuck on the back. $900,000 dollars in advertising failed to get the same traction as these cheap magnets.

How do I know the magnets worked? Good question.

My cellphone number was on the card and I received countless calls after hours and on weekends – it didn't take long to identify the source. Within a few months, the calls trickled in and within a year was a steady flow.
Pluck those blessed harp strings baby.

Working the land is important. The difference between a 40% closing ratio and 30% is an additional 15k-20k per year, *plus* the repeat and referral business driven from the extra sales. Many family providers take second jobs to see an increase like this – something achieved in less than an hour by doing follow up (arched eyebrow).
Prediction: Work your land, prove you can be trusted with after-sale follow up, and something else will happen – spoons (deals that fall into a manager's lap and they give it to whomever he or she wants).
Family members, neighbors, or leads from previous customers are common in a manager's world and the last person they hand free money to is salespeople who refuse to work his or her own land. Fling fairness out the nearest window when handing neighbors, fellow church members, or family member's trust into someone else's hands – they pick security every time.

68

Prospects, which call the store rather than stop in, represent a large portion of harvest. Walk-in traffic engulfs most salespeople and they neglect phone leads. This forgives much fruit.

Consider this:

The year was 2009 and the auto industry struggled from the economy crash sparked by ~~greed~~ the banking and housing crisis in 2008. In spite of this, our dealership did well *but* we weren't exactly stapling help-wanted posters around town. One day I get a call from a fella moving back to our area. Ryan sold for a dealership six hours away and did well and I gambled and hired him over the phone – very much throwing up a prayer that a bright red nose and shiny oversized boots wearing fella didn't show up.
Cue circus music.
That prayer was answered when a bright eyed, eager gentleman stood ready to go Monday morning (deep sigh). Ryan instantly sold vehicles – *many* vehicles. In fact, within two weeks, he caught our leading salesperson and within another week, he topped the leaderboard.
Hmmm... What is going on here?
I'd better plant an eye on his activity. How was he outselling my skilled staff? After all, my team all pulled their weight – zero slouches. I watched to see if he was beating staff

to lot ups – nope. In fact, he wasn't hawking the lot at all. Friends and family deals? No, sir. *Cue head scratching*.

Then it hit me. *Phone leads*.

Ryan sat at his desk and kept a watchful eye on the blinking lights indicating an incoming call and he snagged calls before the receptionist. This resulted in many phone leads, thus converting sales in the process. In fact, in just over three weeks he produced 26 sales. Here's the interesting part: *He never took one lot up!* They were ALL phone ups.

How did Ryan sell so many phone ups?

He knew that vehicles aren't sold over the phone – appointments are.

Phone-up Dynamics – to understand phone ups first we must understand the person at the other end of the line (sensing a pattern?). It comes back to that dinner table discussion when Ma and Pa pass around fried chicken and gravy. Ryan and Claudia set guidelines and then search to meet those guidelines – not exactly brain surgery. Somewhere between "Ryan, honey, please wipe the ice cream off your chin." And, "Sales line two." They make a list of vehicles. Phone prospects have a simple goal: cross your name off or circle it. Circled entries trigger a visit.

GET CIRCLED.

A phone-up never utters: "I'm just looking." That alone makes phone-ups refreshing. Clearly, if a person dials a dealership's Sales Department they intend on purchasing, therefore eliminating a shopper's biggest crutch.

Identify the Caller – meaning collect a name and number. This removes the cloak of invisibility, and people behave differently. Would you believe that some callers find it perfectly acceptable to treat sales staff rudely, and, in fact, notch up efforts over the phone? *Insert sarcasm.* This is part of daily life, and hey, the auto industry certainly earned this throughout the years, so expect bad behavior built by decades of shady salespeople.

"Let me check and see if that unit is still available. Can I get your name and number? I will call you back in five minutes." *Voila!* You just accomplished two important things: Obtaining valid contact info and disrobing the caller. It won't sell the vehicle, but it makes the path less treacherous.

The callback – armed with a name and number, get a full picture of needs. *Cue needs assessment form.* To open additional doors, try this: "We take in many trades and there might be something else that would work even better than the vehicle you called on. Let's go over some details and I'll check for other vehicles, by the way, getting a chance to buy a vehicle before its advertised is a great way to purchase."

Sell Appointments – with a full picture, we move the sale forward. *Not so fast, Champ.* We cannot sell vehicles over the phone – we can push appointments though. After completing the registration form, immediately attempt setting an appointment.

"Can you come in today, or does tomorrow work better?"

Set appointments quarter to, or quarter past the hour. Research shows that appointments set at 5:15 or 5:45 have a greater chance at showing then ones set at 5:30. Use the Or Method to lead shoppers into appointments and narrow your way down to an exact time.

Sales: Does today **or** tomorrow work better for you?
Buyer: Tomorrow.
Sales: Does morning **or afternoon** work better?
Buyer: Morning.
Sales: Does 9:45 **or** 10:15 work better?
Buyer: 10:15.
Sales: Sounds good. I look forward to meeting you.

Whether it is a teacher, customer, or future ~~boss~~ wife "I look forward to meeting you." is a clean way to end calls.

Close your way down the path by asking or questions until you have an exact time. This works well in other areas too. Stack options accordingly and it's a win/win.

❖ Go to bed after reading a book **or** before?
❖ Pick up your toys after supper **or** before?
❖ Go to the park before taking out the trash **or** after?
❖ Rather I build a new race shop **or** new racecar?
❖ Rather I sleep on the couch **or** in my car?

Stubborn Customers – surely, these methods won't work every time? What if when Mr. Squirrely refuses to run right down or even call me back? Fair enough. Casey, one of my better phone-up handling salespeople had a good method for dealing with the stubborn ones.

"Let's walk around the vehicle together,
call me back on my cell phone
and I'll explain it to you."

Watching him reach out, touch scratches, and explain potential issues was amusing. This little dance captures a fruitful incoming call log, but also builds rapport by being upfront about issues. Casey's tactic was simple: Build rapport while walking to the vehicle. Even the toughest cats eventually warm up with enough effort.

Distance from Store – figure out how far the caller is from the store. Handle local prospects differently than callers two hours away. As a rule, prospects are willing drive 1.5 hours for a vehicle purchase. Prospects beyond that range would benefit from a verbal walk-around, price, and payments over the phone.

Mirror Near Desk – smiling is natural when face-to-face but over the phone, we need help remembering. *Um, why?* Messages delivered behind a smile are received better – whether the smile is visible or not. By planting a mirror next to your phone, it serves as a reminder to smile. Besides the two extra scoops of good energy, that mirror might catch a bat in the cave before your customer does.
Roger that, Captain.

What Will You Be Driving? After setting that almighty appointment the last thing you want to worry about which coworker is going to "accidently" (rolls eyes) work with your prospect. Prevent future ~~indictments~~ conflict by asking what they drive so you can keep an eye out.

Make one final request: "My name is Russell, please write it on the advertisement in case it's busy." Armed with a name, this prospect should have no trouble finding you.

Phone-ups are especially eager to dismiss salespeople if they whiff something amiss. Therefore, show you're different from others, and prove it through action. With a few easy strategies, phone-ups can be a great source of sales, and help shape a well-rounded salesperson. Don't shy away from phone-ups because your uncomfortable speaking over the phone, as with everything, repetition is key. I'm confident that if you make a good impression, the caller will give you the first shot to earn his or her business.

We have a little joke about phones in the car business:

We call them cash registers.

Closing Skills

The Road to the Sale eventually coils down to this final resting place: Closing. Let's begin by defining what it means to close a deal.

Think engagement.

An excited fella asks his lady's hand in marriage, she says ~~get off my porch~~ yes and the county finalizes it – both parts are important. To close a deal is the same as getting that girl to say yes before marching into finance and changing the name on the title.

Before hitting finance, the customer needs to say yes, meaning they will buy if certain terms are met such as, price, payment, and trade value.

74

Let us discuss a few methods for getting that yes.

Unlike a nervous boy holding a ~~pregnancy test~~ ring, we close through worksheets – not verbally. Sure, a customer can commit verbally, but take it a step further and have commitments initialed. This informs the Desker, Floor Manager, and Finance Manager that the customer is closed.

We split closing techniques into basic and advanced methods. 80% of the time the simple methods work, so advanced techniques are the exception, not the rule.

Always start with basic tactics and only use advanced techniques if needed.

Always Write Worksheets – whether it is a fresh lead, high school friend, or Uncle Rodney, *always* use a worksheet to present numbers. This retains confidence and prevents mistakes. It's tempting to skip worksheets if we know the buyer but if we veer from the process, we risk forgetting important things. This bites you later on and loses respect of the buyer. *And no,* don't treat Uncle Rodney like a stranger – but use the same presentation process to reduce errors.

Case in point:

James, a new salesperson, searched for a cheap truck for his girlfriend's parents, which lived four hours away. He felt writing up a worksheet wasn't needed and pushed his Desker for numbers on a fresh trade.

Twice, the Desker refused.

"Need worksheet, Mister."

The third time was the charm, finally spitting out "$4,000 plus TTL."

Which he misinterpreted as $4,000 plus their trade. Finance printed the paperwork and he delivered the vehicle. The deal recap (a form showing profit), showed a large profit, rather than the small profit intended. *Hmmm.* This is odd.

Cue nail-biting salesperson.

To make matters worse, the customer totaled the truck right away and the insurance company questioned such a high purchase price.

Does anyone have a towel?

James has egg all over his face. Shame on ~~me~~ the Desker for submitting to a third request for numbers without a worksheet, and again to the Finance Manager for printing paperwork without hard numbers from the desk. *But hey,* neither of us had to sit across from those buyers at Christmas dinner. *That, my friend,* would be the salesperson.

The good intentioned salesperson could've saved a headache by using a worksheet and always present them the same way.

Rebuild Value – before attempting the close, recap the options and rebuild value in the vehicle. List the options down the side of the worksheet and underline the ones that are hot buttons. This reminds the buyer that the vehicle meets needs and helps the Floor Manager if they help close your deal. Sample Ford Explorer list:

4 Wheel Drive	Moon Roof
3" row seat	V8 Engine
Heated Seats	Leather
Tow Package	Non-Smoker

Basic Closes

Move to Payments – most budgets are payment based. Therefore, by moving to payments we speak their primary language. Furthermore, we hold more profit by backing into desired payments rather than negotiating price. Speaking their primary language and holding additional profit both take a backseat to the biggest benefit: *Flexibility*. Payments give Deskers and Finance Managers flexibility on how they structure deals to submit to lenders, which leads to more approvals.

Good grief, can we speed this up a bit?

Alright, Champ, here we go.

Two-Choice Close – present two choices and ask which way works best. This concept is very basic *and very effective*.

0 Down	$219/mo.	_____
$1,000 Down	$199/mo.	_____

Notice what happened here (wink wink). We simplified decision-making, asking to put zero down or $1,000 down, rather than deciding to *accept* price or *accept* the deal. We already knew their payment goal (registration form) and selected a vehicle to meet those goals – therefore, the Two-Choice Close works most of the time. Regardless of which option is chosen the price isn't reduced, which results in more gross profit.

The two-choice close isn't just for payments, with a little creativity we move from if they are going to buy to which choice. Consider a few examples:

- ❖ $14,999 *or* $15,999 With 3 yr. warranty
- ❖ $14,999 *or* $15,999 With four new tires
- ❖ $14,999 *or* $13,999 As is
- ❖ $329/mo. for 60/mo. *or* $299/mo. for 72/mo.
- ❖ $199/mo. *or* $239/mo. and $2,000 in accessories

Ben Franklin Close – this close is effective when dealing with nervous Nellies that worry about making a bad decision. Vehicles are a major purchase, thus creating a need for a little reinforcement.

The close goes like this, "There was a wise man by the name of Ben Franklin who used a method for tough decisions." Turn the worksheet over and draw a line down the middle. Write **Buy Vehicle** on the left side, and write **Keep Trade** on the right side. By now, you should know the customer well enough to help list all the pros to purchasing on the Buy Vehicle side. List as many items as possible and repeat the task for the Keep Trade side – except shut up, and leave the customer to add entries. Assuming the left side clearly outweighs the right – hold out your hand and welcome them to the family.

Buy Vehicle	**Keep Trade**
Better Fuel Mileage	Payment Increasing
Nicer Vehicle	Insurance Increasing
Reliable	Starting Payments Over
Safe Winter Driving	
Under Warranty	
Lower Interest Rate	
Better for Bad Back	
More Passenger Room	
More Seating	
Trade Needs Tires	
Trade Needs Brakes	

This close creates a nice visual, making it clear which side has more advantages, and reinforces a decision to move forward with what they started. *Hey*, they ventured into the store intending to solve a problem, right? Give a little push across the finish line.

The Ben Franklin Close draws on both emotion and logic, therefore finding a home in either type of buyer. The logic sits there in black and white – a nice long list of reasons to purchase. 'Safe Winter Driving' glares at the emotional heart and the 'Trade needs tires and brakes' screams at the logical buyer.

If this doesn't work, there is a strong possibility that the customer landed on the wrong vehicle and you should get a manager involved, or switch units, before losing the deal.

The Take Away – the last example brings forth a common denominator on hard-to-close deals.

Why won't my customer agree to purchase?!
< banging head against table>

This is a legit frustration – so much has already happened and not getting a commitment is a red flag that something is wrong. Make sure that something isn't the vehicle.
Cue test.
Try switching units (verbally), and if they allow it – this indicates that you're on the wrong vehicle. Bounce back to the drawing board rather than push the current vehicle.

Most of the time the opposite happens – no sooner than uttering, "Maybe we should find a different vehicle." and the customer leans forward and makes it known that they want to continue discussing the current vehicle, *which is a very good sign*. Move forward with confidence that somehow, someway, we're on the correct vehicle and go fishing to discover what's hanging the sale.

Go Fishing – refers to going on a hunt to figure out way they won't commit. Such as, damage, smell, or needed service. Perhaps, removing the cash down or kicking the trade is enough to sway the buyer. Eliminate things one by one until you identify the issue.

Sound like a spouse's cold shoulder?

Well, maybe a little. Maybe going fishing aids in more than closing deals? Rumor has it that these tactics help pull out a spouse's frustrations as well.
Ugh. Ok, you win.

I'll sleep in my PJ's instead of my racing suit, but tomorrow, I get to pick.

Lean forward and listen up, an important dynamic happens behind the scene with hard-to-read customers. Not everyone is comfortable negotiating. *Why would they be?* How often does the average person need to barter, wrangle, haggle, debate, bargain, parley, mediate, settle, compromise, quibble, quarrel, squabble, or pull hair over products?

Fear bubbles to the surface in weird ways.

Anxiety, confusion, and tension are all present before throwing in a skilled salesperson. Factor in the urge to grandstand and it creates ~~clumps of missing hair~~ confusion.

Rather than allowing these factors to frustrate, simply chalk it up to indirect tactics by a person not comfortable being direct.

Understand the dynamic and deal with it

Likewise, with hearing NO. Don't give up! When this happens, everyone loses. The dealership loses revenue, which offsets advertising dollars. Service Writers lose new service customers, Technicians lose vehicles to service, the Parts Department loses the ability to provide parts, Sales and Finance Managers lose gross and sales, and the salesperson saws a branch from his or her tree.

The customer loses the most. *Huh?*

Yes, the customer misses out on the experience of getting *you* as his or her salesperson – there is a high chance that whoever makes the sale (if they left) won't take care of them as good as you would have.

Ready to turn up the heat a bit? Follow me.

We tried the Two-Choice, Ben Franklin, and kneeled awkwardly on one knee. She stood firm with her hand planted on her hips:

"Get lost ya bum!"

Next, we swung the Take Away Bat and then went fishing to make sure we are on the correct vehicle.
Cue crossroads.
We can throw our arms up, stalk back to our desk, and watch our beloved customer go on down the road and fall in love with some other eager ~~salesperson~~ vehicle – *or* – dig in and work things out.

Oh, good. You're not a giveruper either?
Grab the shotgun, Pa. We're gunna track us down a weddin'.

3M Close – The 3M close works in situations whereas you have met every demand, and spent a *loooong* time doing it. This close works well as long as two things exist: The correct terms and solid rapport. Correct terms mean price and payment are within goals, and solid rapport means your customer loves you enough to pick you up alongside the road and provide an alibi. You're about to make an all-in bet that the customer likes you, so if he or she doesn't absolutely love you, don't try this close. *Ya been warned!*

Start by turning over your worksheet (blank side) and say, "I'm new, but they tell me there are only three things that stop a customer from making the purchase."

Write **ME** on the paper.

> "Have I treated you guys well?"
> "Yes, Caleb you've done a great job."
> "Ok, then it can't be me."

Draw a line through the ~~ME~~, and write **MONEY**.

> "The payment is within range, correct?"
> "Yes."
> "Then it can't be the money."

Draw a line through ~~MONEY~~ and write **MACHINE.**

> "Is the vehicle everything you wanted?"
> "Yes, the vehicle is perfect."
> "Then it can't be the machine."

Draw a line through ~~MACHINE~~ and circle **ME.**

> "Well than it must be me. I'll find a different salesperson to help you guys out, clearly it must be me."

>> ~~ME~~
>> ~~MONEY~~
>> ~~MACHINE~~

Thankfully, I have yet to meet a customer that allowed me to get up and replace myself (knocking on wood) – this is where rapport stands tall. They don't want to see their hard-working salesperson miss earning money. Furthermore, customers don't want to start over with someone else. *Granted*, if the money is within their goals and nothing is wrong with the vehicle, then what is the issue? *Hmmm...*

To my recruits with large ~~cojones~~ faith, I commend you in advance. *Go ahead now*, put your money where your mouth is, give the 3 M Close a whirl.

Kick Trade Keep Payment Close – we joke about joining customers and vehicles in Holy matrimony – complete with changing the last name on her title, but people really do connect with vehicles, so much so, that it's common for customers to name their vehicles. Interestingly, usually names of the opposite sex. *Hmm...*

These attachments are counterproductive – especially when Petey, Sally, Freddy, or Madison is overvalued.

"What do you mean? Petey is only worth $1,000 dollars?"

Rather than prying a low-value trade out of customer's hands, kick the trade and attempt to close the deal in the process.

"I'm not sure if my manager can do it, but what if you could keep Petey and we kept the same payment? Would you purchase then?" This reduces gross, so keep your manager in the loop before attempting.

If that doesn't work, grab your customers hand, march out to Petey, and explain that if he really wanted to see his owner happy, he would let her go. <sniffle>

As a joke, of course. *Well, sort of.*

Gas Payment Savings Close – use this close on customers that put on many miles and refuse increasing payments by $20-$30 dollars per month. Upgrading vehicles usually means increased fuel mileage, which opens the door to this close.

"Roxy, if I can prove that you can save money by buying this vehicle, would you purchase it?"

"Sure. But I don't see how."

Flip over the worksheet and ask how many miles she drives a year, or do the math on their trade (miles when purchased minus current miles, divided by years owned = Miles per year). Excuse yourself from the table and pull up the government website for checking MPG. Input the trade and new vehicle, and do the math at the table.

Foxy Roxy's deal:
Current vehicle = 20 mpg
New Vehicle = 31 mpg
Miles per year = 15,000
Price per gallon = $3.09

- Trade vehicle = 15,000 (miles driven) divided by 20 (mpg) = 750 gallons x $3.09 = $2,317 divided by 12 (months) = $193/mo.

- New vehicle = 15,000 (miles driven) divided by 31(mpg) = 483 gallons x $3.09 = $1,495 divided by 12 (months) = $124/mo.

- $193 minus $124 = Savings of $69/mo.

"Because the new vehicle gets better fuel mileage, you'll spend nearly seventy dollars less per month less in fuel. Your payment is only going up $30 per month, so you'll spend $40 per month less. Welcome to our family."

Maintenance Close – use this close when the trade had large repairs (PETEY! Pack your things and GET OUT).

Complaints about Petey → Unrealistic payment goal → Begin close during appraisal.

Using the note box, detail Petey's recent repairs (within the last year). The customer assumes they are increasing Petey's value and spill every bit of work done to it (wink). Write a dollar value next to each repair, some of the items will indeed increase the value but we'll be using this information differently.

Continue with the sales worksheet but if you have trouble getting the extra $50/mo. needed, try this:

"If I can show how you can afford the extra $50 dollars a month in payment, would you buy this vehicle?"

"Yes, but I don't see how."

"Your current payment is $227/mo. and you told me that you've spent $1,200 dollars in repairs in the last 12 months ($1,200 divided by 12 = $100/mo.) that makes a combined payment of $327mo., your new payment is only $289/mo. and it doesn't need any repairs, welcome to our family."

Stick out your hand.

Reduction to the Ridiculous Close – again, this close attempts getting $30-$40/mo. payment increase. Break down, or reduce, that additional amount into something relatable.

Our vices suck money out of our pockets (shocker). Mine happens to be dill pickle sunflower seeds (Bigs Brand),

86

Redbull (extra tall), and kissing smiles (wedding ring equipped).

Aim for an easy habit such as, smoking, coffee, energy drinks, morning doughnuts, protein shakes, or candy bars. Don't ask the customer to quit the habit – especially a smoker.
<removing lucky pen from left eye>

"If I can prove that you can afford this payment, would you buy the vehicle?"
"Yes, but I don't see how."
"I noticed that you're a smoker." Frantic eyes searching for nearest weapon, "Don't worry; I'm not going to ask you to quit, but can I ask you something?"
"Go ahead."
"How much is a pack?"
"Seven bucks."
"And how many packs do you smoke every day?"
"One."
"If your habit **increased** to just one more pack a week, could you still afford to smoke?"
"Yes. Of course." Says the eye-rolling customer.
"Well, that's only $28 dollars per month more, exactly what I'm asking. Welcome to our family." Stick out your hand.

This is a nice twist from the assumed direction, they gear up to defend themselves – surely *increasing* their habit isn't an issue.
Use round numbers and break it down to monthly cost so it transforms to monthly payments.
Coffee = a dollar a day.
"If your coffee habit increased to two cups per day, could you sill afford it?" (Extra $30 per month)

Refinance Close – stalled Low-Credit-Score Buyers, please step forward.

Low scores drive high interest rates, which push payments much higher than expected – or wanted. When Low-Credit-Score Buyers object to higher payments it's tempting to let them get educated elsewhere, but doing so costs you the sale. They eventually get educated and come to grip with higher interest rates, and end up buying – *just not from you.*

Hmmm. Silly question. Why don't we educate them? *Well, duh. Nicely!* Start by printing his or her credit report and circle the things that lowered their score, things like late payments, collections, and maxed credit cards. Most people understand how scores are lowered, but make sure they understand how *their* score was reduced.

Please, pass the humble pie.

After disarming sharp attitudes, go to work on their squishy heart.

Are low credit scores a permanent condition?

By *gosh*, no. Therefore, we shouldn't treat it as one. With a little work, credit scores can be dramatically raised – in months, not years, and as a result people can refinance loans into better rates – *wait for it* – which reduces future payments. Give sample payments at a lower interest rate and ask the customer if they are able to pay the higher payment until they can refinance.

Is refinancing an absolute certainty?

No, nadda, and heeell no. Instead, be honest and show the path.   I used to hate the refinance close because I felt ~~slimy~~ crafty salespeople took advantage of buyers who didn't know any better but after letting people go and finding

88

out that they purchased elsewhere at the exact same payment, it frustrated me.

Cue missed opportunities.

The opportunity to make a sale and the opportunity to educate. Educate with these credit tips.

- ❖ **Late Payments**- avoid making payments over 31 days late. 30 days late might trigger a late fee, but it doesn't reduce a credit score until 31 days late.

- ❖ **Payment History** – keep loans open for one year. 12 months of history is more beneficial than paying off loans early.

- ❖ **Multiple Trade Lines** – means different types of credit, such as, credit cards, mortgage, installment loans, lines of credit, etc. Lenders like to see at least five open trade lines to deem the person stable. It's common to see a 700 score and because there are only one or two credit cards in their history they get rejected for larger loans.

- ❖ **Inquiries** – quit allowing businesses to check credit. Excessive inquiries hurt scores. "Would you like a 10% discount today by applying for our line of credit?" Deny these credit inquiries.

- ❖ **Available Credit** (biggest factor) – add the total credit limits and the total balance of all credit cards. Example, $10,000 available credit with $2,000 total balance equals 80% available. When this percentage drops below 65%, it drastically reduces credit the score. Increasing the available credit also increases your score almost instantly (must wait 30 days for credit file to update).   Increase the available credit by paying down balances, increase credit limits, or adding new credit cards with zero balance. These things drive the available credit percentage higher and drastically improve the score.

Many dealers treat low-credit-score customers as subhuman – it is wrong, and finds no home in a Spirit-driven salesperson's heart.

"He who is without sin among you, let him throw a stone."
John 8:7

This verse is one of my favorites. A woman was caught red-handed in adultery and a mob quickly formed. They grabbed stones ready to dish out a death sentence. Jesus intervened. He scribbled words in the sand trying to disarm the mob. Some say He scribbled the names of men who had committed adultery as well – whatever he wrote, it was dramatic because one by one the men dropped their stones and left. The few that remained heard this famous line: "He who is without sin among you. let him throw a stone." With that, the rest disbanded and left.

Salespeople may not be clutching rocks, but the auto industry casts wicked attitudes towards low credit score buyers.

Drop the stones and educate instead.

Giving extra effort builds rapport with these hungry buyers – in fact, enough to land the first sale and many after. They also produce many referrals.
Cue splitting clouds.

1 to 10 Close – this close helps draw out objections. It goes like this:
"If you were to rate this deal from one to ten, one being that you hate it and wouldn't take the vehicle if I gave it to you and ten meaning you'll quit licking the windows and buy it right now, where does this deal stand?"
"An eight."
"What would make it a ten?"

Perhaps, they won't tip over and buy it but you'll identify a hurdle and figure out how to clear it. SIDE NOTE: Any number less than eight indicates that you're on the wrong vehicle and should consider switching.

Closing Tips

No one is immune from frustrating roadblocks, whether brand new, or a veteran with 5,000 fish hanging from the stringer, one thing is certain: Buyers say no. Don't fret about such things – *expect it.*
In addition, salespeople are quick to discount rather than trying to preserve gross. These anxieties reduce gross and even lose deals. *Huh? Dropping price loses sales?* Yup. By accepting offers too quickly, customers feel as if

91

they offered too much and some back out. Avoid this by letting customers feel as if they earned the deal. For example, instead of accepting an $8,000 offer, come back with $8,211.37 – they feel as if they squeezed every penny out of the dealer.

Before discounting, try these tips.

Finance in house – some buyers say their paying cash but actually have financing set up elsewhere. They assume offering "cash" gets a better deal – not true. Lenders share interest rate reserve with dealers so we prefer that everyone finances. Therefore, moving a cash buyer to in-house financing makes a deal that is easier to manage and easier to close. Hang the carrot of low interest rates and zero down financing. Draw out their interest rate and try to beat it (very likely). This helps close deals because the dealership retains control. More than a few bankers sink deals.

Remove Cash Down – sometimes buyers get cold feet about parting with their funds– or lie miscalculate amounts, instead of confessing, they stall. Drop the cash down and it may move the deal forward.

Consult a manager before attempting, as this may reduce gross profit.

Add a Cosigner – request a cosigner and push an indirect choice: Would you rather accept the payment offered, or ask for help? Either way, the deal doesn't lose gross. Most buyers would rather do things on their own and accept higher payments. Either way, you forced a decision.

Switching Units – Are they dead set on a certain payment? And you cannot make it work, then switch units – not to be confused with the take away, which just verifies that we were on the *correct* vehicle. Switching vehicles at the worksheet step means we missed something further back on the Road to the Sale, but sometimes it does happen (especially if the prospect picks the vehicle). Rather than ~~throwing a fit~~ quitting, attempt to sell a different unit.

Re-qualify, regroup, and identify where they can be flexible.

<shaking crystal ball>

I see a high risk of running out of time.

90 Days Until First Payment – another zero-profit-reducing closing tip is offering to push the first payment out 90 days. As with other tactics, simply laying it on the table doesn't work. Set it up. "I'm not sure if my manager would do it, but what if I could get them to push your first payment out 3 months, would you buy the vehicle?" If agreed, write it out on the worksheet and have it initialed, doing so still holds the team effort of you and them against the store, and because salespeople aren't decision makers this tactic still holds water in the honesty bucket.

0% Interest Rate – use on buyers with excellent credit scores. WARNING: This tactic won't make any friends in the Finance Department. Some lenders allow the interest rate to be bought down by the dealer – even on used vehicles. For example, if the buyer qualifies for a 2.35% rate, some lenders allow the dealership to pay all the reserve upfront and write the loan at 0%. This tactic will cost your deal gross and produce scrunched up eyebrows glaring staring through the Finance Manager window.

The 800+ Credit Score Buyers are the toughest to close and this close could be your key.

Good luck, Mate. You'll need it.

Round tables – sitting behind a desk sends a clear message: YOU V.S. ME. Ding – ding – ding. Intended or not, sitting behind a desk is an aggressive stance.

Avoid this by working deals at round tables.

We're a team.

Complete registrations, appraisals, and worksheets shoulder to shoulder with prospects.

Our closing axe has a nice sharp tip, let's move on to our next skill.

Product Knowledge Skills

Product knowledge frightens new salespeople. *Why wouldn't it?* Thousands of makes, models, and trim levels intimidates the veterans and beginners.

> *What if they ask an odd question, and I don't know the answer? Will they think I'm a ~~weirdo~~ fraud?*

Whatever your concerns are, I promise that you're not alone. Realize two things: Everything discussed before now is more important, and learning product knowledge at a slow pace is okay.

Before clamping our head in the product-knowledge vice, let's wrap our head around people.

Does everyone communicate the same? *No, Sir.*

Process information the same? *No, Ma'am.*

People are time-tellers or clock builders; the former is good at communicating the time and the latter is good at building clocks (shocker). Each type gives and receives information differently. The average customer doesn't demand to know how a clock is built, they want the time:

94

Clearly and cleanly. In fact, customers grow frustrated when questions spark a barrage of tiny details.

"What kind of rims are those?"

"Aluminum." The time teller responds, but a clock builder starts forty steps backwards.

"When it was molten liquid.... therefore, it's 17% aluminum, 43% byproduct, and 40% highly ~~irritated~~ enriched prospect."

Imagine if every "What time is it?" question encountered "Well the secondary gear is at a 45-degree angle, which meets the primary gear, which swings the...."

"*Please*, just tell me the time!"

High producers know which hat to wear and when, and most days the time-teller hat trumps the clock-builder.

Being direct controls the tempo, moves the sale forward, and avoids running into the ditch. We've focused on people not products – because understanding people is more important – *much more important.*

New salespeople can still produce income knowing nothing about vehicles and pickup skills as they go. Just like tools in a toolbox, we pick up knowledge from others and use it when needed.

Think garage repairs.

What happens when we get stuck? We borrow tools or knowledge to figure it out, right? The same thing applies to oddball product questions – walk over and borrow knowledge from a veteran salesperson and put him or her back when finished. *Easy peasy.*

Here is a three-step system that will bulk up your product knowledge muscles.

Step 1: Makes and Models – "What is a Buick?" Stop in front of each vehicle and name it: Ford F150; Chevy Silverado; GMC Sierra; etc. Once you can name them (without peeking at the side or back), you're ready for step two. This may be little more than a memorization exercise, but that is okay.

Estimated time: Two hours per 100 ~~beers~~ vehicles.

Step 2: Trim Levels – things get a little harder here, but well worth the effort. Every vehicle has a trim level: Basic, mid-grade, or fully loaded. For example, a Ford Taurus comes in SE (basic), SES (mid-level), and SEL (fully loaded). Every model uses a system just like this: Good, better, best.

Time telling.

Understanding trim levels is a short cut. By recognizing SES as a mid-level trim, we can skip trying to remember every little option upgrade and say, "This is a mid-level vehicle." In contrast to rattling off all the upgrades from a basic trim level. To my head-shaking veterans, *yes, eventually* we learn this information, but we are still in Basic Land. It's fruitful to push product knowledge things off until they are easier to digest.

Learn your brand first, if you sell Fords, focus on Fords. If Chevrolet then focus on Chevrolets, and if Dodge then focus on Dodgaronies.

Grab your lunch pail. We're headed back to the lot.

Stop in front of every Ford (or your vehicle line), armed with a cheat sheet in the back of this book, and list all the trim levels associated with that vehicle. Start with basic and list all the trim levels up to loaded.

For example, stop in front of an F150 and list every trim level. "This truck comes in XL (basic), STX, XLT, FX4, and Lariat (loaded)." Move on to the next Ford and list its trim levels as well. Skip all the specialty trims such as King Ranch, Raptor etc. Stay simple and focus on the core. The goal here is to sum up a STX by saying, "It's a basic model, but a step up from bare bones." *Time Telling*.

Next, tackle engine and cab size. Most trucks come in regular cab (R/C), super cab (S/C), and the largest available – crew cab (C/C). Stop in front of each vehicle and list its trim level, engine size, and cab.

Hang in there Champ; it's easier than it sounds.

Then expand to competitive makes, meaning if you sell Ford learn Chevrolet and Dodge as well. If you sell Honda then learn Toyota and Mazda. Most dealerships stock inventory for their direct brand and a few competitive makes. Ford, Chevrolet, or Dodge dealerships won't stock foreign vehicles, and a Toyota, Honda, or Mazda dealerships don't stock domestic vehicles.

This weeklong exercise builds a solid base and carries you until further training.

Step 3: Manufacture Videos – every manufacture produces product knowledge videos. These videos highlight the areas in which their vehicle outshines the competition, complete with a ~~deranged~~ high-dollar spokesperson to stoke the fire.

Every dealer has a room with a TV, DVD player, and a stack of these videos high enough to cast a shadow to the nearest coffee pot – which you'll need plenty of to finish the video marathon. *Cue jitters*.

Dealers with weak training throw a box of these videos at new recruits and call dem trained up. Woe to the dealer that considers this training – but it does serve a purpose: New Car Buyers. The videos cover the current model year, and focus heavily on improvements over last year's model or the areas they beat the competition. Manufacture Cool-Aid sure does taste good but it risks information overload. Therefore, it's last on our training list.

What about shoppers whom wet themselves hearing about every little detail?

Instead of grabbing a mop bucket, grab the product knowledge guru and ask him or her to help. This doubles as a learning opportunity. Eventually the goal is to handle any situation, but this is a great starting point - gurus were once green peas too and owe karmas wheel a push or two.

In addition, Truck Buyers already know more about trucks than 90% of salespeople, so fall back and let them crawl all over the vehicle. Just keep them confined to the walk-around step.

Danger lurks with added skills: Product knowledge doesn't sell vehicles – rapport does, so never shortchange rapport and overcompensate with product knowledge.

Walk-Around Skills

ALL ABOARD! Next stop: Walk Around Land. Help me drag this beast across the stump, would ya? We're going to chop it into three easy parts: Basic ~~idiot-proof~~, one to grow into, and one that would make a politician blush.

98

While you're slipping your mittens and moon boots on, please allow me to tell a little story.

Early in my sales career, I worked for a sales team that helped dealerships run events. Once a month, our sales team dressed up in suits and ties and ~~beat our chests~~ had a meeting at a 4-star golf course, which, by the way, is the closest I ever want to be to putting greens, I get along with golf clubs slightly better than an ice pick does with a block of ice.

The meetings were high energy and a great venue for leadership to wrap arms around the team and make sure our ~~strait jackets were fastened~~ we were on the same page. Leadership spent half the time pushing our motivation button and the other half covering scheduling needs.

The meetings began at 9 a.m. and ended with a basic lunch buffet, which served chicken, fish, and steak.

The atmosphere was upbeat and motivating, but after a few months, the buffet lost its draw. We simply had gotten used to every dish.

One day, Jeff, the team owner invited our spouses and changed how the buffet was served. Rather than handing our plates and pointing to the serving line, the chef came out, apron and all. "Good evening ladies and gentleman, I'm Scott, Turtleback Golf Course's head chef." He wheels out the buffet and pauses in the center of the room.

"We've prepared a special meal for you today and before you begin, I'd like to take a minute and explain our dishes." Scott, a lanky fellow that looks as intense as any seasoned college professor, pauses and gathers every eye in the room.

He walks over the chicken, lays a piece across a plate, and turns towards the group. "We stuff our chicken with thyme, inject butter under the skin, and finally add two pierced lemons before roasting. It's important not to overcook the chicken so we constantly baste it with juices." Scott pauses, and one could hear a pin drop the room was so quiet. The group waited. The silence waited.

Next, Scott plates a piece of fish and turns back to the group. "The fish is marinated for eight hours with a paste made from ginger-garlic and rice vinegar. Before baking, we add cayenne, turmeric, and salt. After it's perfectly seasoned, we carefully cook it and finally top it with a half of lime. He continues to hold every breath in the room and confidently displays the meats with one hand and his other hand acts as his voice's extension, dancing along with his words.

No one has moved an inch.

Meanwhile, Scott plates a slice of shaved steak and turns towards the group, ready to explain the last main dish "We're very proud of our steak, and like anything done right, it's not easy. First, we tenderize it through a three-day aging process. Next, we give it a dry-brine and rub it with garlic. To seal in flavor, we sear each side for exactly sixty seconds before placing it on a rosemary bed and roasting it for 30 minutes. I think you'll be surprised on how much flavor this process retains.

Scott, gently sets down on the side of the buffet and takes a second to explain the wild rice and the side dishes. "We thank for your business and look forward in taking care of your future needs." And with that, Scott disappears.

The result was profound.

The buffet shifted into something very different. Chef Scott turned chicken, fish, and steak into something I couldn't do myself, making it unique. This uniqueness turned into eating something special, and transformed that meal into a better dining experience. The first to rave about the buffet *specially prepared for us*, were the spouses. Groups buzzed about the taste – clearly impressed. Team members also ate slower as well, identifying the things they liked best, and finally, my own reaction surprised me the most. I leaned over and asked my wife which one was her favorite. The interesting part:

It was the very same buffet as previous meetings.

Did Jeff intend to give his staff a lesson on presenting? *Perhaps.* Impress thy spouses? *Maybe.* Regardless, that dancing chef flicked a light on between my ears. Through simple presentation, we greatly alter perception, and giving attention to detail increases our products value. *You too*, can change perception by simply taking time to explain vehicles.

Do we deep dive every option? *Yaaaawn.* No sir.

Tell time and hit important points. Scott didn't tell us about how the farmers raised the chickens, or how fisherman clean fish. That's clock building. He told time. Short, sweet, and informative – yet took enough time to show he cared.

Years later, I heard that Scott had never presented his dishes before and fretted about doing so, in fact, he practiced for an hour before we arrived. I enjoy that part the most – knowing he resisted doing it, yet absolutely nailed it. He worried about stuttering and communicating well (in front of salespeople, no less), yet I watched a roomful of people rave about a meal that would've been skipped had our spouses not been there.

It's worthwhile to mention that I've reconstructed Scott's words – I clearly remember his effect over the group but don't remember his words verbatim.

So how do we utilize the same concept with vehicles?

Lead customers around vehicles and build value, explain features – *and fingers crossed* – transfer excitement. Reach back to the needs assessment and connect specific needs to the vehicle's options. This completes the circle and reinforces a decision to purchase, inch by inch, we move the sale forward. Transferring excitement is an art form – shoppers, like diners, relish excitement and yearn to find a vehicle that provokes the little kid within. Turn up the volume and make an impact through bright eyes, voice inflection, and glowing energy.

The Auto Industry is littered with staff that refuses to present vehicles – most toss keys, point to the vehicle, and limp back inside.

Hmmm. Sounds like an opportunity.

Rochelle test-drives a Ford F150 at Dahlberg Motors and leaves to shop around. She finds another one at your dealership, except you do an amazing walk around, explain the features, and explain how those features benefit her. Haven't you created an advantage over the competition? *And how much does it cost? Zero.*

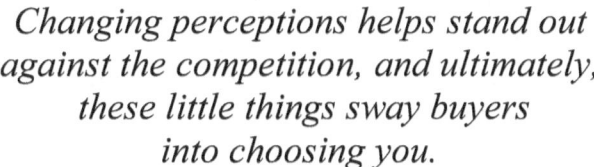

*Changing perceptions helps stand out
against the competition, and ultimately,
these little things sway buyers
into choosing you.*

Hot Buttons – are points, or issues, that are important to prospects. Identify them, and push those buttons throughout the sale process. Our first opportunity is during the walk-around. Things such as, fuel mileage, seating space, safety, size, brand, leather, moon roof, towing capacity, horsepower, cargo area, etc. are common hot buttons.

Get to know your customer and avoid talking about irrelevant things. For example, our Soccer Mom's pitch wouldn't include horsepower, aggressive body lines (the van, not her, *ya jerk*), or zero to 60mph capabilities. On the other hand, a 22-year-old mustang shopper wouldn't hear about seating capacity, legroom, or trunk size. Both would shoot a blank look, tilt their heads, and say, "Who cares?" These are extreme examples, yet every shopper has unique hot buttons to aim at, and others to skip entirely.

Silly question, mate. What would happen if we tried having a conversation with an excited eight-year-old in the middle of a county fair? I'd bet a 4-scouper ice cream cone, jumbo cheese curds, and an awkward pony ride that his or her attention is severely divided – if given at all. In the same way, shoppers struggle to keep their eyes off the shiny vehicles.

Prevent distractions by moving the target vehicle away from other vehicles. Have the prospect wait inside and pull the vehicle to a secluded area, and then follow a set walk-around prep process.

> → Pull vehicle out
> → Brake hard to remove brake dust
> → Park where customers don't have to use reverse
> → Pop the hood and trunk.
> → Slide driver's seat back (forces person to adjust)
> → Tilt steering wheel up (forces person to adjust)
> → Open all doors. hood, and trunk

This process prepares the vehicle for the walk around, not the actual walk around process.

Good grief, are we there yet?
Yeah, yeah. Quiet in the back.

Walk Around Process – tackle a walk-around through process. Start at the same point; move around in the same direction, and finish at the same location. A pre-organized plan helps display greater confidence and prevents missing sections.

Walk around process:
> → Front bumper
> → Underneath hood
> → Passenger side
> → Front brakes
> → Passengers side doors
> → Passenger side rear seat

→ Trunk
→ Driver's seat
→ Interior options

SIDE NOTE: If the customer shows any sign of disapproval, discontinue walk around!   Checking watch, looking away, shaking head, or puking on the sidewalk indicates a need to switch direction.
Continuing kills rapport.

Swiss Army Knife Walk-Around (Basic) – this walk around fits every vehicle built in the last 20 years, from a Chevy Aveo to top dollar BMWs.

1. **Front Bumper** – "This vehicle is fitted with a five mile per hour impact bumper designed to withstand low speed hits, which minimizes damage and avoids tripping the airbag system.   The aircraft-quality headlights are designed to withstand high-speed rock hits.   The rounded lenses are designed to see 30% further into the ditches than the older style."

2. **Under Hood** – "Everything you need to monitor is clearly marked with colors: Oil cap, dipstick, coolant cap, and power steering cap." (There are many other things under the hood, but our basic walk around identifies the very basics).

3. **Passenger Side Front Wheel** – "This vehicle has front disc brakes and an ABS system designed to stop quicker than drum style brakes because they disperse heat better and have a computer system to prevent wheel lockup under heavy braking."

4. **Passenger Side Doors** – "This vehicle has 5000 pound per square inch side intrusion beams that run the entire length of the vehicle, which helps prevents punctures in accidents." Sit the customer in the back seat. "This vehicle has theater style seating that allows passengers to slide their feet under the front seat and sit high enough to see out the front window. Adult passengers enjoy viewing the roadway."

5. **Trunk** – "Notice how large the trunk is? This vehicle is fitted with trunk hinges that don't crush the contents inside the trunk, which provides more usable space."

6. **Driver's Seat** – Sit the prospect in the driver's seat and kneel at the doorway. Point out features on the driver's door panel: Power locks and windows, power mirrors, power seat switches. Close the door and hop in the passenger seat. Once inside, continue pointing out features such as, fingertip controls, heater controls, and the radio.

Congrats, you just did a basic walk-around. Even though it's *veeery* basic, it's still better than most of the competition and applicable to 90% of vehicles roaming the road today. Notice that many statements began with, "This vehicle has...", even though these features are included in every vehicle made in the past 20 years; in fact, the department of transportation mandates most of the items.

This is like the chef who explains his or her dish.

The Swiss Army Knife Walk-Around tackles even the most complex vehicles with ease. Do we use advanced methods? *Sure*, on familiar vehicles, but unfamiliar vehicles engage the Swiss Anny Knife rather than tossing keys.

Let's lean our ladder against a better walk around.

Tag & Receipt Walk Around – we add tags and receipts to the presentation, which draws feedback and helps get them involved. Use the same process: Start in the front, then passenger side, swing around rear of vehicle, and end up in the driver's seat – add short questions, called tags, and when the shopper gives an answer, it's called a receipt. Ideally, pick questions that are specific to needs, or hot buttons.

Buyer: Kobe is trading his Ranger for a F150 and we identified his hot buttons as, extra seating room, towing capacity (concessions trailer), better gas mileage, and upgrading to a fully loaded vehicle (loves leather).

1. **Front Bumper** – "This F150 has the EcoBoost engine, which gets over 20 mpg. It would be pretty nice to tow that concessions trailer with ease, and yet get good fuel mileage while buzzing back and forth to town, wouldn't it?" (Tag)
   "Yes it would." (Receipt)

2. **Passenger Side Doors** – "This F150 is a crew cab, which gives rear passengers full doors and the most leg room out of any F150 offered. It would be pretty nice to load everyone into one vehicle instead of having to take two, wouldn't it?" (Tag)
   "Yes, I hate taking two vehicles." (Receipt)

3. **Driver's Seat** – this truck is the top of the line Lariat Model, which gives it leather and heated seats. Leather looks newer longer and opening the door five

years from now and seeing sharp interior would be nice, wouldn't it?" (Tag)

"Yes, my friend Elijah has a truck with leather in it and it still looks brand new." (Receipt)

"Coming out to a warm vehicle in freezing weather is one benefit but my customers really like being able to control the comfort level without quarreling over the heater controls. The heated seats combined with dual temperature controls should settle a few fruitless arguments, wouldn't you agree? (Tag)

"Sure would, I can't remember the last time I won that battle.' (Receipt)

Would salespeople that skip a needs assessment be able to do this walk around? *Um, nope.* They come up short and either have to explain every feature, or toss the keys and skip it. The former drains precious sand from the hourglass and erodes rapport by spitting out irrelevant details. *Ish.* Prospects don't decide to purchase all at once, it happens over a series of events – internal "yeses". Customers don't speak these yeses aloud; they click them off inside their hearts and little by little.

- ✓ *Oh good, this vehicle has enough seats.*
- ✓ *The fuel mileage is exactly what I am looking for.*
- ✓ *Perfect, it has heated seats.*
- ✓ *How nice, my salesperson isn't ignoring me because I'm female.*
- ✓ *Oh, good, the paint is the same color as Rice Lake Speedways walls, better to hide the scratches.*

The customer accepts the vehicle little by little and a wise salesperson clicks those mental checkmarks off until confident that they have enough to close the sale. Our emotional side is ready to pull the trigger like Elmer Fudd hunting wabbits, but our logical side reaches over and clicks the safety until convinced.

Top Shelf Walk Around – pull up the shotgun barrel, lets aim at New Buyers.

Time to point out where our product is better than the competition or last year's model. Manufactures spend millions testing vehicles and figure out which points outperform the competition, and then stoke the fire around those specific points.

Watch manufacture videos and use those selling points in your walk around. Your prospect has likely researched and heard some of the very same points emphasized.

Do ya smell that? Yup, rapports sweet scent.

Auto manufactures wage war against competitor's vehicles ever year (shocker). Sometimes indirectly through advertising and other times tweaking tests to find a way to ~~cheat~~ outshine a rival. These videos are the result of all those factors coming together. Manufactures spend millions to plant messages in the very ears of the people who handle the almighty customer: Salespeople.

I fell so used.

1. **Front Bumper** – "Notice the styling with Ford's new grille and headlamps – Ford's new face really stands out. Quality gleams, even at 50 mph coming in the opposite direction. Ford did a great job letting others know that quality is barreling ahead."

2. **Underneath Hood** – "This truck comes in three engine configurations: Six-cylinder EcoBoost which gets over 20 mpg, a Triton 4.6 V8, or the industry

leading Triton 5.4 V8. This truck engines beats both Chevy and Dodge in..."

3. **Passenger Side** – "The F150 has a fully boxed in frame that mounts shocks outside the frame rails. What happens to your inside wheels when cornering? The body rolls and causes inside tires to lose grip, which reduces traction. Mounting shocks outside the frame rails reduces body roll, enabling this truck to corner like a wide-track car. The other manufactures still use old C-Channel frame rails that twist and turn under load. Over time, that twisting weakens metal. Ford built you a truck that will withstand years of industrial grade abuse."

4. **Rear Seat** – "Hop inside. Notice how much room your feet have? Ford's team of top designers did a great job at getting those rear seats up nice and high. This provides a ton of legroom. Our rear seating is bigger than..."

5. **Truck Bed** – Ford is the only truck that installed steps both on the side and rear tailgate, which is great for getting inside with your hands full or simply being able to reach over the side without having to climb inside. This truck has tailgate assist, which includes hidden coil spring that helps you lift it. Feel how light that is? It's 50 pounds heavier than previous older models. Ford built you a better tailgate, but thought far enough ahead to make it easier to use. Our truck bed is held in place with bolts three times larger than...."

6. **Driver's Seat** – have a seat in America's best-selling truck. Notice how everything wraps around the

driver? The dash and controls are a cockpit-inspired design that wraps controls around the driver. Notice how the controls are in the same area as your old truck, yet they have done a great job upgrading the..."

Game. Set. Match.

Consider yourself equipped to role-play your new walk around skill. After 20 sessions (each), you're ready to bark fire and go live.

The biggest factor luring people back to the same brand cycle after cycle might surprise you: Control placement. Regardless of upgrades, manufactures wisely leave the placement of common controls alone. Things like, wiper, radio, heater and AC controls usually stay in the same locations because manufactures know customers will ~~pen nasty letters~~ refuse learning them, buyers reject vehicles with unfamiliar controls. *Hmmm.* What better way to hold customers? *Moowaa ha ha haaa!* Reassure buyers that these items were left alone during the walk around.

This example is from many years ago, and purely for structure, not content.

SIDENOTE: My extended family eats, sleeps, and throws rocks at anyone whose lips formed the words Ford, pro Chevrolet all the way. So, when I started managing a Ford store, I felt a little – how does one say it – *adulterous.* Working at multiple franchises exposed me to every product line, which developed open-mindedness for each manufacture – but settling into a Ford store didn't feel right.
Mister, ya done took things too far.

Then something interesting happened: Mike Rowe, Ford's high-dollar mouthpiece. Yup, I fell into the box of product knowledge videos, which pumped up Ford's products six ways from Sunday and crawled out of the promotional river soaking wet.

Cue Buy-in.

My words matched my heart and recommendations followed. Anyone care to guess what brand of vehicles I see when pulling into family gatherings (besides Harleys, mopeds, and painter horses)? You guessed it – many rock throwers now own Fords. *Some,* I would have never guessed.

Pretty low, even for a Bowtie Brat.

Looking back, if that video box had been labeled Honda then those rock throwers would be driving Hondas, and if Dodge I'd been staring at Dodges (and tow trucks) but I bought in and that's all the mattered. To be effective in New Franchise Land then you must buy-in as well. Youngsters adopt their beliefs and love parroting adults when knocking on brands.

Should adults parrot their youth? *Hmmm.*

As a salesperson, I chuckled at folks that were just like me before selling vehicles: "I had an 84' Ranger once and it was a pile of donkey dung. I'd never buy another Ford." All manufactures produced vehicles that underperformed, and judging products based on technology used 10, 15, or 20 years ago is ~~foolish~~ fruitless.

After selling over 6,000 vehicles, I've grown to prefer a certain type of vehicle as well: *The ones with familiar controls.*

Be careful sloshing through the Promotional River because danger lurks behind Mister walk-around celebrity's sparkling eyes: Information overload. Each model line has its own videos: Compact cars; midsize cars; large cars; compact SUV; midsize SUV; large SUV; (*deep breath*) small truck; half ton truck; and one ton truck is a normal product lineup for the major players. Videos only cover that model year, meaning they roll out new videos every year.

Anyone smell brain cells searing? Sheesh.

Save this activity for last because it's more important we know how to sell than what we sell.

OVERSELLING WARNING: Oversellers, folks who proclaim the vehicle being shown is "absolutely perfect", risk a tricky situation. *And no,* I am not referring to lies or exaggerations. Lies are never the answer and doing so is like dumping hot coals over the Holy Spirit's head.

"Let yes be yes, and no be no."
Mathew 5:37

But, *why?* Shouldn't we set the hook – the deeper the better? *Well Champ,* what if the shopper doesn't like it? Is the next vehicle perfect as well? Sounds a little foolish to label every vehicle God's divine vehicle, doesn't it?

Overselling hurts creditability. Ease into presentations and gauge reactions before pushing your chips in.

Then throw the tickle machine into gear.

If the vehicle matches needs *and* connects emotionally, *then* we have something to work with.

Fuel Mileage Questions – commonly emerge during the walk around. Resist redirection – running off to get the manufacture rating is counterproductive. Give a range instead.

"Low to mid 30's"
"Mid to high 20's"

Besides staying on the Road to the Sale, we give a better answer. A vehicle rated at 32 mpg doesn't mean drivers achieve 32 mpg. *Huh?* Hang with me here. Factors such as, quality of the fuel, driving style, winter months, and tire inflation reduce fuel mileage. Up in the Northwood's (eh), we leave vehicles idling, which reduces fuel mileage drastically.

Silly question: If we tell Kyle Busch that his Chevy Aveo gets 42 mpg and his math shows 12 mpg, who is Kyle giving the finger to? His lead foot or his salesperson? *Oh, OK.*

Any disgruntle letters about author's choice of Kyle Busch for example will be used in Thunder Valley's porta-potties. Research shows that Kyle Busch material cleans bottoms better than two out of three leading brands of toilet paper.

The effects of doing a great walk-around are additional gross and an easier customer to close. We want to build so much value that the customer is embarrassed to ask for a discount.

Perhaps, a touch farfetched, but what a great goal.

114

Chapter *Four*

Developing Attitudes

In May of 2007, I accepted Managing Partner position in a Ford dealership and found myself working with a high percentage of senior citizens – a slight change of pace from the working-class younger people (bruises from umbrellas instead of research folders). Different buyers required different rapport building questions.

How about two birds with one stone?

Perhaps a newlywed should seek husbandly tips from nature's best source: Old married men. And while we're at it, I'll take two scoops of common ground. *Mmmm mm, my favorite.*

"What's the secret to making her happy?" I'd ask.

"Things just get easier after 10 years," or "I just let her be right." Followed by smirks and winks.

Cue bullshit answers.

The real answer surfaces after she walks away. They lean forward and say:

> *"She knows I'm grateful to be the one who gets to take care of her."*

Over the years, this statement snuggled within my heart. A wife who feels cherished responds differently, thus creating an endless loop enjoyed by both parties.

Um, what does this have to do with sales?

Everything.

Salespeople court prospects, and prospects pick their salesperson (sound familiar?). Salespeople hunt for the next buyer and neglect the ones already landed. *Pretty low, even for a ~~womanizer~~ salesperson.* During the sales process, salespeople respond to issues quickly but after-sale issues see much slower feet, which leaves that less-than-cherished feeling.

> *"If I then, your Lord and teacher, have washed your feet, you also ought to wash one another's feet, for I have given you an example."*
> **John 5:14-15**

Jesus led with a servant's attitude and we should strive to match it. Will there be days when taking care of issues is inconvenient? *Or, hey* – just plain don't want to do it? *Uh huh.* Without a doubt.

Replace I *have* to – with – I *get* to.

A cherished customer responds differently. He or she gives leeway on mistakes, grants time to locate vehicles, or my personal favorite: Brags to referrals. Referrals such as these wait hours just to work with you (oh dear, I think I just wet myself). This level of service starts with wanting to be *their* servant.

2006 marked a life-changing year. I joined team that ran dealership events. They spent 10-20k for four days of advertising and then hired us to handle the extra traffic. We traveled together, ate together, roomed together, and of course sold together.

The team had an outstanding reputation, known as the best around – often selling more vehicles in four days than most stores do in an entire month. The team fired on all cylinders and had great culture – so much so, that people felt it instantly upon entering the store. The existing dealership staff, our own team, and the shoppers sensed something special in the air.

Nothing-Negative Attitude – Leadership's first lesson: A *Nothing-Negative* Policy. Managers didn't allow staff to say anything negative about coworkers, the dealership, customers, or themselves. They were so committed to the Nothing Negative mantra that even if someone said something negative back at the hotel a teammate would lean over and say:

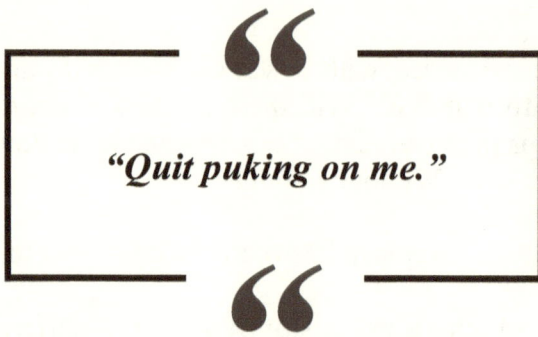

"Quit puking on me."

Rephrasing negatives is the first step into a newborn spirit.

Things such as:

➢ "My customer stinks." Rephrased, "My customer has stable employment, at a hog farm."

➢ "My customer is a jerk." Rephrased, "I have a very direct customer."

➢ "The snowstorm is killing traffic." Rephrased, "Prospects that show up will be serious buyers."

➢ "My boss just pelted me with a snowball." Rephrased, "I need to lock the bathroom door while going number two."

We rephrased many negatives, but even more were never uttered. This produces a better environment because we step around irritations and protect attitudes.

Failure riddles the Sales Industry, so keeping a positive outlook is no easy task. As mentioned, the average closing percentage is a meek 30% – we expect failure seven out of every ten times. Left unchecked, this leads to a negative environment very quickly.

Want proof, grasshopper?

Fill your pockets with two handfuls of ~~bullets~~ patience and venture into a few dealerships and observe attitudes.

Very few *feel* right.

Often, negativity is the culprit – snuffing out environments, attitudes, and production everywhere.

It takes a little work, but forming a Nothing-Negative Attitude tilts the world's energy and it reacts to you differently – its forces show indirectly. Prospects take notice and feel confident about doing business with the right person, and send referrals your way – fruits multiply when those referrals send more.

Pluck those harp strings, baby.

Coworkers notice and assist you when needed, or protect your interests when you are not around. Decision makers, i.e. da boss, recognize a deeper level of buy-in and much fruit accompanies a boss's good graces. All these things accompany a Nothing Negative attitude.

Quality VS Quantity Attitude –

*"It's the quality of time at work,
and the quantity of time at home that counts."*
- Brian Tracy

How does one improve the quality of time at work? Question every task! Especially tasks that eat into family time after hours. "Is this task more important than doing XYZ at home?" very rarely does that answer produce a yes.

Hey! What about providing?

This requires time away! *Yes, agreed.*

This Balance frustrates many people, and it has no preference whether you're a horse or pony, sprinter or crawler, lover or fighter, seasoned vet or a newbie.

*"But if anyone doesn't provide for his own,
especially for those of his household,
he has denied the faith and is
worse than an unbeliever."*
1 Tim 5:8

Ouch! Well put, Father. This verse hits the responsibility nail directly on its head – *yes*, providing means work.

However, what else does providing mean?

Well, families cannot live on bread alone – perhaps it also means providing structure, discipline, and encouragement. Maximizing time at work is a key attitude to become a high producer *and* a family leader.

Dump unproductive things by creating a Stop-Doing List. If a task isn't directly growing the customer base, protecting the customer base, or a direct order from management than it has a high probability of being fruitless.

> *"Every healthy tree bears good fruit, but the diseased tree bears bad fruit."*
> **MT 7:17**

Poor use of time leads to unhealthy habits, which eats the trunk and infects the entire tree.

Fill your day with things that produce good fruit.

Specifically, complete petty tasks during slow hours. This prevents eating into family time later on. High performers comprehend this concept deeply. In fact, just try to pull them into a fruitless conversation and you'll get front row seat to a less-then-courteous exit. These cats work under a different set of guidelines – sideways conversations become habits. *Cue exit.*

I clearly remember the day I began excluding myself from sideways conversations. I paused, tilted my head like a confused dog, and left. Within a week, I no longer had to do that much.
Sound cold?

It's warmer than the plate of food waiting at home, much warmer than the missed bedtime stories, and certainly warmer than being replaced (get my drift).

"The next day starts the night before."
-Author Unknown

Research shows that for every 10 minutes spent planning for the following day saves an hour tomorrow. Our short memory span tricks us. With the day fresh in our head, we neglect writing the following day's to-do list because we're convinced that we can pick right up where we left off. The next day we struggle to remember the important little details, as a result, we sp sp sputter. What happens when a prospect surfaces? *Yup*, we shuck everything to the side and help them, which starves the hanging issues even more.

Planner entries:
- ✓ Calls to make — (add phone numbers)
- ✓ Appointments — (add phone numbers)
- ✓ Vehicles to get ready

Next, reject pocketing everyone else's problems. Raise your hand nice and high if your pockets are already packed. *Yup,* me too.
Shhhh, can you keep a secret?
There is big difference between a sounding board and agreeing to solve problems for others. Salespeople are natural problem solvers and relish figuring things out. *Be careful!*
One Minute Manager Meets the Monkey, by Ken Blanchard does an outstanding job with this metaphor. Imagine your problems as monkeys – perched on your shoulders and constantly jumping around knocking things over (Your Honor – *it was the monkey* — I swear). Everyone

has their own monkeys and stress about them. When people complain about their monkeys, be careful not to leave with the little squirt, meaning agreeing to take care of their problem. Repeat this activity across multiple people and life is filled with chasing everyone else's monkey.

<hiding the hair gel>

Here lies the secret: Be careful at the end of conversations because that's when problems get transferred from the griper to the listener. A "helpful" person risks managing everyone else's monkeys and severely limits their ability to handle their own monkeys.

Hey buddy! Aren't we supposed to help each other?

Helping others, neighbors, and even enemies is at the core of Christian Principles – but there's a fine line between assisting others and completing people's work. Provide advice, resources, or clarity instead of taking projects over.

Teach man to fish, or give man fish? Oh, ok.

In contrast, quantity of time is what counts at home – simply being available when life's lessons present themselves *provides* for the family. Workaholics must be very careful about their hobbies. If time at home is limited and we pick up a hobby that removes us yet again, we are in serious trouble. Instead, find hobbies that include family members.

Hey, don't look at me like that! If a toddler sits on a bucket, they can see out the front window of ~~his~~ my racecar.

One of my biggest regrets isn't striving harder to find this balance. *Cue Fathers forgiveness.* Neglecting time at home sends ripple effects through the household that extra paychecks digits fail to overcome. Abandon home life long enough and it bares its teeth and sinks them into your work spirit as well. Protect both areas with a Quantity and Quality attitude.

Take all Deals Attitude – commissioned employees have a nasty habit about not chasing small profit deals, or ones they *think* are small (rolls eyes). This is a horrendous mistake. Initially, it costs lost revenue and missed referrals but surely also causes bad vibes and prevents future deals through word of mouth advertising.

Why come back to a place with bad vibes?
Why not ~~tattle~~ tell others about the experience?

Let's review how most low profit deals happen.
> ➢ Putting too much money in a trade
> ➢ Unforeseen repairs
> ➢ Market fluctuation
> ➢ Aged inventory

All these issues push cost beyond normal. Salespeople that are fussy about selling low profit deals cut their own throat in the form of discouraging the store from being aggressive. *Foolish.*

On the other hand, some salespeople don't feel right about high profit deals. Just like owning a vehicle too high there are times when a dealership owns a vehicle lower than normal, things like:

> ➢ Repairs were less than expected
> ➢ Buying a group of units for a better deal
> ➢ Market value increases rather than decreases

Why should we forgive additional profit in these cases? Isn't there a need to balance low profit deals?

124

The Auto Industry operates with very low profit margin percentages, meaning profit as compared to a percentage of total sales. A $500-dollar profit on a $20,000-dollar vehicle is only a 2.5% profit margin. Shoes, clothing, electronic, services, and many other industries enjoy much higher profit margin percentages. The dealership has many expenses.

How are those expenses paid? Through Profit.

Care to guess what the biggest expense is? *Employees.* Without profit, everything evaporates, including employees.

In comparison, the state charges a 5%-7% sales tax on every vehicle sold – often profiting more than the dealership, and if the dealership loses money – guess whose waiting with an extended arm? No one bats an eye about paying sales tax – and the state has zero invested into vehicles, people, or the light bill. *Errr!*
End rant.

Let swing back down Take-All-Deals Lane. The answer lies with a simple, yet very effective, system: The Thirds. At the end of every month, our deals should sift into three buckets – high, medium, and low. Meaning if we sold 100 units, then 33 should be low, 33 medium, and 33 high (or close).

In addition, reaching for every deal creates more deals – *a lot more deals.* Attempt high profit, use gross-holding techniques, yet be willing to take a near zero profit deals.

Amazing. Things. Happen.

What qualifies as a high, medium, or low deal? Great question. The average profit is $1,500, so medium deals compare to the market average.

Use this system:
- ❖ $2,000 or higher = high
- ❖ $1,000 - $2,000 = medium
- ❖ $1,000 or less = low

When it comes to how much profit is acceptable, everyone has a different opinion. Some salespeople turn up their noses unless its $4,000 and some salespeople sell 20 vehicles and never make over $1,000 – both miss income they could enjoy by adopting The Thirds attitude.

Stop fussing about profit
and let the cards fall where they fall.

The almighty customer deserves to be viewed as a person who trusts you with their needs first, and profit second. Ironically, in doing so, you'll pocket more money through increased volume.

Friends and Family Deals - Consider this common scenario:

Jacob sells a Ford Explorer to his mother for $20,000, which is $150-dollar profit. Jacob looks at a small commission check and feels content. *Why make money on my mother?* Little does he know, but the dealer owned the car wrong and she paid $1,000 over market average.

Elijah sells his mother an identical Ford Explorer for $18,000, and is upset after seeing $1,500-dollar profit, he marches into his manager's office, and throws his commission check on the desk. "What the hell is this?! You knew that was my mother!" In contrast to Jacob's deal, Elijah's mother paid $1,000 under market average because the dealer owned the vehicle well.

This scenario is a tricky one.

Has Jacob treated his mother better just because he only made $150 in profit? Is Elijah a Class-A jerk for turning a $1,500 profit on his own mother, even though she paid $2,000 less than Jacob's mother?

Here lies the answer.

Don't be more concerned about what the dealer paid than what your loved one has to.

Want to help loved ones get a good deal? *Great*, I'm onboard. Let's make sure they are pay under the market average and take things a step further and ensure that we communicate the vehicle's condition.

Failure Attitude – High producers treat failure differently. The average struggler fires up the blaming machine and fuels it with everything under the sun.

- The inventory stinks
- Finance isn't working hard enough
- The prices are too high
- They were just looking
- My underoos restrict the blood flow to my brain

Struggling salespeople throw these stones and a pile of others. In contrast, high performers' figure out where they went wrong and try not to make the same mistake twice.

"I just haven't figured out a way to sell them – yet."

Clear-cut errors sting the most. Letting prospects leave before discounting is a common misstep. Finding out they purchased down the road for a few hundred dollars less produces ~~gnashing teeth~~ scrunched eyebrows. Failure to hit a payment goal and not digging for a cosigner, only to find out they purchased down the road with one is a tough pill to swallow. Whatever mistakes you make, *and there will be many*, don't let them spin you out, *Fail Forward* by vowing never to repeat the same mistake twice. The fastest way to learn is through failure. Carry a Mistake Book and track major mistakes to learn faster.

The format is simple:

Mistake Book				
Date	Name	Unit	Mistake	Cost
3/18	North	Exp	Tried holding too much gross	$480
5/25	Newman	Focus	Didn't ask for Co and she bought elsewhere	$500
6/26	Manor	F150	Didn't identify decision maker	$500
7/7	Dahlberg	Ram	Discussed Politics and lit dudes fuse bad	$100
10/2	Swartz	Ram	Discussed Religion and customer bolted	$150

Healthy failure attitude: Each failure is one-step closer to making a sale. The Law of Averages inches up with every new prospect. John Maxwell from *Failing Forward,* recommends viewing falling down not as failure – just one step closer to your goal when you get back up.

By Failing Forward, you protect your best asset: Your attitude.

> *"How much better to get wisdom than gold,*
> *to get understanding is to be chosen rather than silver."*
> **Proverbs 16:16**

Using a Mistake Book helps us gain wisdom by pausing and reflecting when we mishandle situations. Recognizing our mistakes, especially the ones within our control leads to self-accountability, something rare in the auto industry. Many salespeople start the finger pointing within seconds after a deal falls apart. "Finance dropped the ball." or, "The desker screwed it up.", or, my personal favorite, "We cannot compete with the big city dealerships." The bigger the dealership, the more expenses they have and they must produce more profit to cover those expenses!

These salespeople are in grave risk.

Instead of changing their behavior to produce better results, strugglers chase their tail and play the blame game. Trace *all* mistakes back to your own actions. Sometimes identifying the mistake is easy, like realizing you didn't identify the decision maker – clearly the salesperson's fault. Other times, tracing takes a little work. "We ran out of time and they had to go." Is this the desker or appraisers' fault for not working fast enough?

This sends many sales dogs barking. *Hmmm....*
Is this really a healthy attitude?

How would a self-accountable salesperson view this problem? *Well...* If I had better rapport the prospect would

130

have stayed. Or, "If I would've done a better job priming them for wait times, they wouldn't have grown frustrated."

Every time something negative happens, salespeople should blame themselves?

Seems a bit, extreme. *Agreed.*

However, looking inward creates a much healthier environment. Granted, *some* issues are indeed others fault, but in most cases, a good salesperson can overcome the sins of others.

Consider the stats.

On average, we fail seven out of every ten attempts – failure is expected. Why turn these expected failures into friction points? Why allow yourself to be spun out 7 out of every 10 attempts?

Once perfected, this healthy attitude bears much good fruit in other areas. For example, the deck contractor builds a desk that resembles a little rascal's tree house – mismatched wood, half-hammered nails, and not a square angle throughout – it's easy to tongue lash shabby work, but does that prevent future construction blunders?

- ➢ Perhaps I should have checked previous work?
- ➢ Perhaps, a half-price estimate wasn't the best option.
- ➢ Next time that smell Mad Dog 20/20 on the workers breath, I will say something. *Yikes!*

By turning criticism inward, we grow. *And, No,* blindly accepting unacceptable work isn't the message here. One needs to find balance between healthy communication and self-reflection and *together*, they combine to produce personal growth.

Dealing with Problems Head-on Attitude – what is the best way to deal with problems?

Head on. Directly. Honestly.

The Auto Industry bulges with people who reject this attitude, and consequently tarnish a great industry. *Ya dirty birds*. Let's review two salespeople dealing with a common problem.

Jason checks his messages Monday morning and listens to Scott complaining about a funny noise coming from the front of his Ford Explorer that he purchased 45 days ago. Jason's dealership has a 30-day warranty, so he knows the issue isn't within the window. Rather than calling Scott, he goes about his day. A week passes before getting another message – considerably more heated this time. *Well, duh*. Jason makes a note to call him, but gets entrenched in a car deal and doesn't.
Hmmm.
The next morning, Jason's manager wants to know what is going on with Scott's vehicle because he got an $800 bill for new brake pads, calipers, and rotors after Scott got it repaired elsewhere. Jason's manager is ~~furious~~ irritated about the bill because he knows it's common for shops to over-repair if they know someone else is paying the bill, yet minor compared to the other problem: An upset customer.
<shudder>
Jason's manager is in a tough spot. Does he refuse to pay the bill because of the 30-day policy? Paying for another shops work is highly frustrating, but 15 days is petty, and he knows it.

In contrast, Kayson gets to work Monday morning, listens to the same message, and immediately returns Scott's call.

"I'm sorry to hear that you're having problems Scott, these darn things are machines and machines break down, but before we get too worked up let's get the Explorer into the shop and see what we're up against, and we'll take it from there."

"I won't have to pay, will I?"

"That's my manager's call, but I know one thing – they are fair, and I'll be involved the whole way. Can you bring it down today, or does tomorrow work better for you?"

As it turned out, Scott had a pebble stuck between his rotor and brake pad – making a squeal. It took more time to get the Explorer on the lift then it did to make the repair. The manager offered to pay the bill but Scott refused because he realized it wasn't the dealerships fault.

Dealing with problems head-on provides better control. In addition, we're different from other dealerships.

Problems provide an opportunity
we wouldn't otherwise have gotten
– proving we deserved the sale.
-C.J. Penn

By being assertive, we prove we're worthy of his or her business. Dealerships spend thousands in advertising to get shoppers to walk on the lot. In fact, the average dealer spends $200-$400 (I've seen as high as $1,000) dollars in advertising for every vehicle sold (not a typo), so when issues surface most managers justify spending a little extra to retain future business – *or best-case scenario* – telling others how they were treated.

Furthermore, ignored repairs become bigger issues. Scott's problem might've grown and because a different shop handled it, we'll never know if the issue was the dealer's fault. Avoid this at all cost, get problem vehicles in ASAP – day, night, or after hours.

Vehicles are machines, and machines have wearable parts that eventually fail – accept this as a certainty, and if the Service Department missed a needed repair: Accept this as human imperfection. There was only one prefect person and He died on a cross over 2000 years ago. The service department only produces revenue by making repairs, so it's a good indicator as wanting to fix problems. Normally, over-repairing is more common than under-repairing.

Repairs are not the only important areas to address head on. Lender denials and high interest rate payments are another source of trouble. Prospects spend half a day waiting for lender approvals, run out of time, and have to go to work. If finance fails to get an approval, or payment is too high, it creates ~~pissed off prospects~~ uncomfortable situations. Don't leave customers in the dark – get with finance and make it clear on who is to contact the customer – *wait for it* — and then do so accordingly.

Handle payment bumps directly. Try an insurance analogy: "Interest rates work like insurance premiums – accidents cause rate increases. When drivers avoid trouble – eventually rates go back down. After some good pay history, the next loan will be at a lower rate." Or, do your best at putting fate back in their own hands through sparking a co-signer mission, which effectively produces a choice: (a) lower payment through a cosigner, or (b) a higher payment without one.

~~Hiding from~~ Avoiding tough situations leads to venting in many ears: Current customers, future customers, and the person that signs your paychecks. *Yikes.*

Other issues fall into this bucket as well: Waiting repairs, ordered accessories, new vehicle orders, ordered parts etc. These common issues should have processes, but problems hang when there is confusion about who contacts the customer. Prevent this by communicating with coworkers and take the bull by the horns and make sure *someone* is contacting them. In the end, they are your customers, and you have the most to lose – so get involved and stay involved.

In closing, how a person handles issues reveals character. Managers look for red flags, which indicates the level of trust they will grant – and handling issues is a massive indicator. With that being stated, handle issues directly and honestly.

Clean Cars, Cost More – in a perfect world, vehicles stay fresh after their bath. Test drives, service loaners, weather, and about a million other things bruise a proud vehicle after the hard-working detail department spends hours applying mascara, foundation, and pulls up her leggings...

Clean cars, cost more. Translation: Clean vehicles before showing to increase its perceived value. *And no*, don't toss the keys to the buried detail department. Roll up thou sleeves and give her a quick five-minute wash yourself. This shows that you care, increases the perceived value, and scores points with the detailers. Detailers don't bring home the biggest paychecks but take great pride in their work. They appreciate someone who also takes pride and willing to their hands dirty. *Cue future favors*.

Use the Clean-Cars-Cost-More attitude during appraisals as well. Give your prospect's trade a quick bath to squeeze more money out of the appraiser.
Did ya see that?
Yup, a halo just formed over your head.

The Attitude of Now! – The attitude of pushing to do things now, in fact, *right now* will serve you very well.

Consider this:
Cassandra pries out Bills needs with a thorough registration, great walk around, and spends extra time making sure he understood the worksheet. They agree on numbers, and wait for finance to finalize the deal. Bill gets a call and tells Cassandra he will return the next day to finish. Cassandra believes that she has done everything right and trusts Bill to come back – they shake hands and Bill leaves.
Bill misses his delivery appointment and Cassandra has trouble contacting him, many unanswered calls litter the following days – sparking Cassandra to ~~sob in the bathroom~~ give-up.

Months later, Cassandra sees Bill in the service waiting area and ~~grabs her shank~~ chats him up, naturally, the deal comes up and Bill says that he fully intended to come back but a different salesperson contacted him and he saved $300 on an identical vehicle. Cassandra wishes him well and strolls through service. The vehicle didn't have a moon roof, heated seats, and had 20,000 more miles.

Identical vehicle? *Hardly.*

Push off deliveries and this story will be your own.

Master this through a Do-It-Now Attitude. If a manager pushes a deal to the following day, well, there isn't much you can do about that – 9 times out of 10 it starts with the customer, they convince the salesperson, and the salesperson sells management.

Don't step into this share.

Many things carry the potential to ruin the deal. For starters, the competition doesn't stop contacting prospects just because they're working with you – in fact, they turn it up, *all the way up.*

What do you do after finding out your customer landed on a competitor's vehicle?

Momma didn' raisum no fool, boss. We's gunna push like hell. Make no mistake; some very crafty salespeople are targeting your customer. Especially if the prospect inquired about many online vehicles and are tangled in many follow up systems. Within days your customer has rabid dogs on his or her bottom – nipping to close a deal anyway they can – as a result, your prospect will become someone else's customer.

Next time dealing with, "I gotta go, I'll be right back." Try this: "While here, you're my customer, but once you leave you'll be anyone's customer. We've gone through so much that I'd hate to see you starting over with someone else. Give me a few more minutes to finish this up, and I promise to do a good job as your salesperson. Is there something that's making you uncomfortable?"

If they need to leave for work? Try this: "I noticed that you make $15 dollars an hour, I'd like to buy 2 hours of your time." Flop $30 dollars on the table. This tactic triggers many calls telling a boss they are going to be late.
Amen.

Likewise, with missing trade titles, paystubs, and proof of insurance. Even if it means following customers home to collect needed items.
Really?
Well, no, not *everyone* needs to do this (insert sarcasm). Only the salespeople that like having deals buttoned up and prefer avoiding slamming their heads in doors due to frustrations. Only *those* people should be concerned about chasing for needed items. It's tempting to wait for the customer to bring them in, but unless retrieved, the vehicle isn't sold yet – dubbed a hanging deal, and hanging deals hang more than finance paperwork – they hang commission checks too.

Adopt a Do-It-Now Attitude, which controls your own fate, and protects your future through avoided frustrations. This attitude bears good fruit in other areas of life as well: Church, home, and ~~last lap passes~~ projects.

Unrealistic Customers Attitude – one can sponsor a NASCAR team on income produced from working with customers that other salespeople refuse. Shoppers come in, are registered, told they are unrealistic, and kick them out like a date that refuses to shower.

What is an unrealistic customer?

❖ Shoppers that lick the windows of a $350/mo. vehicle and expect to purchase it for $200/mo.

❖ Folks that owe thousands more on his or her trade than its worth, and want to keep the same payment.

Hey, wait a minute. Don't dealers advertise such things? *Well, I never...* Perhaps, we shouldn't blame shoppers for biting our hooks. To meet the advertised specials, shoppers need great credit scores, money down, and a long-term loan. People don't read the fine print and seek the same terms without good credit, cash down, and owing more than his or her trade is worth.

Come to think of it, If Christ himself filled out a credit app, most finance guys would come out, set His application down, remove their glasses, and break the bad news: "Jesus Christ, do you have someone willing to co-sign your loan? It shows here that you're an unemployed carpenter, and the ad clearly states you must have a job."

Him, I, and 99% of the rest of us don't qualify for the terms advertised.

Why chase people out of the dealership? Instead, land them on a vehicle closest to their goals, submit to lenders, and present options. Some will scoff (perhaps turn a table or two over), but many will buy. It's amazing how flexible people become after seeing staff work hard on their behalf.

If I still have any egg on my face, kindly remove it please and thank you – *secure that man's advertising pencil immediately!*

Do you recognize a disconnect? Dealers advertise to put prospects within reach and then ~~lazy~~ fussy salespeople blow off the people that show up!

Alex, gimmie commonsense for $200.

Why bother spending the money?

Educate buyers instead. First, salt their mouth by showing a vehicle. Next, take 10 minutes to do a walk around and a short test drive. Then, tell him or her that you will get the lowest payment possible. Finally, bring water through presenting options and use basic or advanced techniques to close. Treat everyone as a neighbor and with respect.

He who has never made mistakes should be the first to boot a customer off the showroom floor. *Ouch!* Refusing to work with less than perfect customers shows an ugly side that has no place in a Spirit-driven salesperson's life. In the end, these customers are rewarding to sell to because of the level of gratitude after the dust settles. Care to guess what activity follows a prospects grateful heart? *Yup,* referrals. The very same headaches deliver blessings through bringing in friends, family, and co-workers because they have confidence in your ability.

Sheesh – send my ~~trophy~~ ribbon to Poskin, Wisconsin. *Please and thank you.*

140

Budget Car Attitudes – a stigma revolves around budget vehicles. It stems from a high risk of future problems. Cheap vehicles are bound to have issues (shocker). Some salespeople don't know how to sell vehicles that have existing issues and others don't like dealing with buyers who are tight with money – both figuratively and literally. Throw in lack of mechanical knowledge – shake vigorously – and *voila!* We have a buyer that many are not willing to tackle.

The term budget car is messy so let's clean it up, if a vehicle meets any of these criteria, it's a budget vehicle.

- ✓ Over ten years old
- ✓ Over 100,000 miles
- ✓ Under $3,000 cost (not price)

FULL DISCLOSURE ALERT: This topic holds a special place in my heart (*awwww*) because growing up its all my family ever drove (*errrr*). $5,000-dollar vehicles were considered nice – *really* nice. Well, Champ, I grew out of that attitude but never ceased wanting to help shoppers that cannot, or will not, buy nicer. *Ah, yes, nothing like a confession to cleanse the Spirit.*
Quit lookin' at me like that bud, we got work to do.

Thousands of budget sales helped develop a great system, let's review it.

Switch – attempt using their funds as a down payment. Financing with a small payment often makes more sense than driving a budget vehicle home. Selling a 70,000-mile vehicle rather than one with 150,000 miles – especially with 15° below zero winters, feels better. The buyer also builds credit; paying cash doesn't accomplish this. Better credit opens better doors in the future – nicer vehicles, nicer home, and lower-rate credit cards just to name a few. It also plants an indirect message: "I didn't want you to purchase the cheaper vehicle." if an after sale-problem surfaces. We're not allergic to future issues, but it sets a healthy tone: We presented better options and they choose differently.

Total Funds – if switching fails, then establish how much cash the buyer has, *exactly* how much. Unlike regular buyers who work within a range, many budget shoppers say $3,000 and forget about tax, title, and license fees. Don't make the mistake of landing on a $3,000-dollar vehicle and then receive a blank stare regarding fees. Ask how much total cash is available and then act accordingly.

Hold Profit – if the vehicle needs an immediate repair, the manager is much more likely to cover it if there was initial profit. Short deals are tolerable, but losing money is ~~too close to the unemployment line~~ another matter. This is exactly why friends and family deals should hold a little money as well – taking care of potential after-sale issues.

Point Out Flaws – overstate potential problems rather than understate and be thorough. Pull out the inspection sheet and review it with the buyer – address problems head on. Review issues that were noted and not fixed, then give a timeline that repairs should be made. For example:

➢ "The tires passed the safety inspection but I recommend replacing them before next winter."

➢ "The inspection shows that the upper ball joints have a little play in them. I recommend changing them before installing new tires or it would eat them up. Our estimate shows a cost of roughly $400."

142

➤ "The brakes passed the safety inspection, but the pads are over half used, I recommend replacing them within a year."

Managers walk a fine line regarding budget vehicle repairs. One hand keeps cost low enough to keep the vehicle sellable and the other hand fixes safety items that cannot be overlooked, which forces a choice: Do repairs, or send to auction without any additional costs. Wholesaling removes the chance to create a customer, earn a commission, and marking another notch on the leaderboard.

Whoa kid, chill.

Let's obtain customers rather than auction checks.

Mechanic Lookover – request their mechanic, or trusted source, to look over the vehicle before purchasing. *Really?* Yeah, really. Keep in mind that mechanics are paid to find issues no matter how minor they may be – so don't get offended when a list returns with the vehicle.

Life's full of choices, bud – give two: Price as-is and one repaired.

We sold 300-400 budget vehicles per year and had very few issues because of these techniques. First, we attempted a better sale, hedged problems along the way, and when major issues came up, we took advantage of the opportunity to help out – which at times meant going right back to step one and taking the vehicle in on trade. The extra deal was appealing, but the real reward was creating lifelong customers.

My final plea: METAPHOR ALERT:

My adored wife trusts me with important things, I've purchased rental properties she never looked at, re-financed loans with little input, and bought enough vehicles to fill Wal-Mart's parking lot – ten times over. When she sends me on missions, I proudly fetch her stick, sometimes its big sticks, and other times its little ones, but regardless I want to be *her* fetcher.

What if she told me her SUV was dirty and I sent her to the neighbor? How about rubbing her aching shoulders, back, and neck at the end of a tough day?

Should I refer the neighbor as well?

Doesn't this carry an undesired risk? The risk of losing my adored wife? *Yikes!* Don't get me wrong, I trust my wife entirely, but I still like to protect my ~~sanity~~ interests.

Wait for it – refusing to work with budget buyers is the same as the foolish husband that allows another man to take care of his wife's 'lesser' needs.

Does this make sense?

After selling the Perkins family ten vehicles, we send them elsewhere to buy a budget vehicle? *Fooooolish.*

If we send a prospect, or worse, an existing customer elsewhere, we risk losing all his or her future business. Not all salespeople are slugs, there are good-looking, honest, and hard-working salespeople to ready to sweep your precious customer off his or her feet and treat them good enough to fetch all their future sticks – new or budget.

End rant.

In closing, everything covered goes deeper than simply attitudes – the way we operate creates mojo and change the way we emit energy. This mojo, or invisible energy, is felt before a word is ever said. We connect with others in so many ways: Emotionally, physically, and

144

spiritually and this mojo gives a massive head start on building rapport.

Cue sales magnet? Yup, that's right.

This snowballs into something much greater than selling vehicles. Others notice and want to be a part of the things your involved in, which cycles back around to create more good things. Our Creator calls this: Multiplying fruit.

Let us talk about protecting that fruit.

Chapter *Five*

Protecting Fruit

Well-roundedness doesn't happen overnight. Much work goes into learning new skills, developing attitudes, and understanding dynamics. Perhaps, they only take a few months to learn, but mastering them takes years. All the while, momentum builds and our production becomes very impressive – enough to justify adding additional hours, responsibilities, and workload. *Cue blessings.*

Just as momentum's fruits multiply, so do dangers that threaten a crash. Imagine a racer that goes on an all-out assault. They install a great setup for every track condition, perfect driving styles, and stick a healthy horse underneath the hood. It works. Solid finishes produce smiles and high-fives. Adding racing fuel jumps the racer out to an early lead often and everyone is happy. They have so much fun racing that they neglect working on the car in the garage. Seasons pass and results stay strong until one day the car breaks and slaps the wall coming out of turn four.

The car is totaled and the driver injured.
In the same way, salespeople neglect self-maintenance. The excitement of selling and competing

146

covers many blissful days and we become like the racer that plants high-fives on the crew, yet refuses to plant energy on maintaining a healthy lifestyle. Neglected areas, such as physical health, spiritual health, and relationships team up to chip away at the high producer and over time cause undesired consequences.

Balanced Lifestyle – physical health, healthy relationships, emotional health, community involvement, job satisfaction, and spiritual health combine to produce a balanced lifestyle. Deep diving these areas are beyond the scope of this book but let's do a quick touch on each.

Three keys to Physical Health: Exercise, sleep, and nutrition. These things help avoid chasing energy in unhealthy ways, thus protecting things far more important than Caesars coins – *our relationships.* Natural energy keeps a person plugged into others at a healthy level and keeps relationships strong and interwoven.

Preserving natural energy helps preserve relationships.

Combining exercise with something you enjoy doing makes it much easier to get motivated. A few quick workouts during the week is often enough to get the blood pumping and keep excess weight off. My beach-less belly grew from shoveling Redbull and gas station food down the hatch until the VW Beetle sued me for design infringement.

Um, yeah.

Timothy Ferris, from 4-hour Body, recommends high protein meals, staying away from flours, fruits, and avoid drinking calories. *Roger that.* Covering the sales floor and eating healthy are natural enemies. Sneaking away for a quick bite is followed with: "Would you like fries with that?" Instead, pack meals. Eating 30 grams of protein right after waking up does wonders to curve binge eating throughout the day.

Sleep is our last ingredient to natural-energy soup – poor sleep forces us to compensate upon waking. Coffee's draw sounds enticing but like any other energy substitute ends up causing a crash. This up and down cycle is hard to break. Avoid sweets or exercise before bed helps prevent tossing, and turning. Still struggling? Get up and ~~scream~~ complete a task. Crossing things off a to-do list helps to mentally shut down. If your struggle is deeper, then consult a doctor. Trained professionals can solve sleep conditions and result in waking refreshed rather than feeling like loaded diesel bus struggling to get uphill every morning. We spend thousands on hobbies yet are frugal about things far more important. Treat sleep as a priority.

Combining exercise, nutrition, and sleep creates boatloads of healthy sale-producing energy.

Healthy Relationships – begins with the person you have chosen to share your life with, your spouse. Devote one night a week as a date night – don't wait for a break in schedules – prearrange a babysitter and find something to do together. No money, no problem. Be resourceful and find zero-cost activities. Keep bills and other friction points out of the mix and catch up on the little details busy couples miss throughout the week. Pay the babysitter extra to handle the tornado that surfaces whenever parents leave so you can enjoy each other more upon getting back home rather than picking up. *Cue slow song.*

Communication issues lead to havoc.

- Aggressive Communicators run others over and eventually look around to empty rooms and matching hearts.

- Passive Communicators avoid conflict to "take the easy route", which creates more future – work, much more. *Cue endless stress loop.*

- Passive-Aggressive Communicators (think sarcasm) send unclear messages. Thus, confusing and offending others.

The goal is to be assertive, which means standing up for your beliefs without offending others, which creates a fruitful cycle.

Healthy communication → Positive response

The female spirit has always ~~made me look stupid~~ perplexed me. Regretfully, I spent years with my head in the sand. One day it hit me: Self, why ignore this complex issue? Racing frustrations launch an all-out assault trying to figure it out. Countless books, you-tube videos, and phone calls to successful racers help to understand the chunk of metal – yet, I am lazy about figuring out my Wife?

Silly question, which has a greater impact on life?

Only a fool to claims to have mastered the female spirit but after standing on a few good books, I can at least look her in the eye. Books like *The Five Love Languages* by Gary Chapman, *The Way of the Superior Man* by David Deida, and *Men are From Mars and Women are From Venus* by John Gray give great insight in understanding spouses.

Emotional health is about paying attention to the things that produce anxiety or other unpleasant feelings and working to eliminate them. *Sippy-cup throwing toddlers? Um, no –* they are blessings!

Labeling anxiety helps keep strong emotional health, which took me 35 years to do. Waiting in the dressing room before a boxing match used to create enough anxiety to burst a light bulb. Later on, long after removing the mouth guard, I noticed the same hair-raising tightness when certain situations came up. Not recognizing anxiety made me feel as if it was uncontrollable – not true. Working out, writing. and prayer all extinguished my anxiety. Be resourceful and figure out causes for anxiety and methods to relieve it.

Community involvement is already the goal of a high performer because of prospecting needs, but let's cover the other side of the coin: Giving back. Karma's scales work for or against us, so it's important that we dedicate time and energy to tip those scales in our favor – *and no*, stroking a check to your favorite church or charity falls under tithing. This is like buying school clothes but turning up thou nose about helping with homework. *Yikes!*

Work satisfaction is a main ingredient to a balanced life. What happens when the clock-builder spends all day telling time? What about the time-teller that clutches fistfuls of hair while trying to build clocks? Both are frustrated, carry tension home, and disperse it across loved ones – causing loved ones to respond poorly – the very people that heavily influence our emotional health.

Accepting a job (or conditions) that brings constant frustrations threaten much more than nightly headaches – it threatens to destroy the family. Combat this by diligently seeking work that is fulfilling as well as a good fit for your personality style.

Our creator built us differently because He knew that it takes all personality types to keep His world running in harmony. *Cue divine plan.* We produce much fruit when lining up our personality gifts with our line of work. Corinthians chapter 12 helps figure out our spiritual gifts and countless online tests help identify our spiritual and work strengths.

Spiritual Health trumps all the others combined. The goal of a spiritually healthy Christian is to live and operate in a way that is pleasing to God.

*"Every tree that doesn't bear good fruit
is cut down and thrown into the fire.
Therefore, by their fruits you will know them."*
Matt 7:19

The serpent looks to bite the spiritually weak and our sinful desires constantly push us off path. Protect your spirit through daily prayer, daily scripture, attending church, and surrounding yourself with others that are spiritually strong as well.

It is written that personal intimacy with God happens through prayer – behind closed doors. Withdraw from the day's frustrations and grant God a teachable heart through prayer. Request wisdom rather than fixing circumstances. In addition, find peace through asking Our Creator to view things from a different heart. "Lord, please show me the next step." Big problems are hard to wrap our hands around, so address problems one slice at a time.

Family prayers give a glimpse into the hearts of those around us – helping connect at a deeper level. Furthermore, it sets a clear example of where our faith lies: In God's hands.

Dedicate prayer time before bed and during meals. Lead with gratitude. There are blessing all around us – adults understand these things much greater than children do. Use prayer time to create lifelong habits of gratitude.

Attending church keeps our spiritual tank full. God gifts His spirit through church and preachers. He blessed preachers with the ability to inspire and ignoring this outlet weakens our spirit. In addition, church members help hold others accountable, like a Shepard that watches his sheep so are church members who watch over each other.

It is written that if a believer witnesses someone heading off path, they are to approach him or her and express concern. Repeated behavior means grabbing a fellow church member and both expressing concern. Failure to change behavior means heading to church leaders.

What a profound system.

We wrap our arms around fellow sheep and show them love – caring enough to get involved. Teaming up with others keeps the rebuffer in check too. This system cuts off pettiness and addresses serious concerns.

Use the same principles in the dealership. If a fellow coworker does something harmful than express concern directly to that person, if that doesn't work than involve a coworker – assuming the coworker agrees – you both express concerns. Additional high-risk behavior means involving managers. Silly question, Mate? *What's the difference between tattling and feedback?* Intentions.

A tattler intends to harm and feedback intends to protect. Protect the person wandering off path; protect the business; and ultimately protect yourself through preserving your environment.

Regular Doctor Visits – Do you expect customers to call us about a funny noise on their vehicle? *Of course*, get that sucker in here ASAP. Keep problems small, right? A health-minded person should do the same with his or her doctor(s). Ignoring check engine lights risks disaster. Addiction, depression, and slew of other things hide within little warning signs.

Leave problems at the door – helps keep focused while at work. Just like a parent who trickles work frustrations home, people drag home problems into work and dissipate it across coworkers. This creates the same cycle: Bring in problems; puke on coworkers; respond poorly; further bad attitude; further negative response – eventually decision makers take action to protect the team. Combat this cycle by leaving problems at both doors – home *and* work.

Mentorship – protects fruits in two distinct ways: Avoiding landmines and sheltering. Landmines litter the sales industry: Customers, coworkers, and managers leave the biggest craters – avoiding these landmines does wonders for keeping spirits high and moving in the right direction.

Would my married crowd please step forward?

How much quicker would learning your complex spouse have been if you had had an old wrinkled up hand guiding your decisions? Would it have cut your learning curve in half, or a third?

Good grief, hell yes.

Mentorship steers around landmines and keeps production high. *Don't hawk over the Finance Managers shoulder – she hates that. I know your shift ended at 5 but they are shorthanded, you should consider staying. Don't worry about him – he's stressed out every Monday.*

These little things add up to a significant advantage. Granting a voice to others is a massive compliment. *I trust you.* This level of trust reciprocates many fruitful things. Sheltering is one.   Sheltering is a byproduct of good mentoring. Once a mentor is convinced of your level of buy-in, he or she will co-sign your future opportunities and then protect you through those opportunities. Case in point:

Jamaar, a great homebuilder, takes pride in his work. One day Jax shows up at Jamaar's jobsite looking for work.   Jamaar, impressed by his eagerness, gives him a job. Jax hangs on every word he says and picks up the concepts and quickly. Soon he tackles tough projects and works on his own. The longer they work together the more Jamaar trusts him. Together, they produce many high-quality projects and build a great reputation along the way.

Through the grapevine, Jamaar hears of a company looking for a foreman and recommends Jax for the position. He hates to see him go but respects his work ethic.

Even though they no longer work together Jamaar regularly stops by Jax's jobsite and looks over his work and continues teaching him on different facets of the industry that Jax hasn't faced before. Jamaar contacts city inspectors, plumbers, and electricians to make sure Jax meets building codes. This sheltering prevents Jax from making mistakes he would have otherwise made – effectively protecting his fruits.

This analogy is my own path in the auto industry. My mentor softened my hardened heart, taught me on the job, recommended me to run my own store, and then sheltered me through continued teaching and kept a watchful eye on my activity.
Cue thankful heart.

Our Creator speaks much about hardened hearts throughout the bible – attributing them to much grief. The bible defines a hardened heart as the un-teachable one. Mentorship allows your heart to be softened, or taught, by a trusted source. The first source is through Jesus's divine teachings throughout the bible, but we also need guidance in our direct line of work as well.

Mentorship propels careers by shortening the learning curve. Mentors redirect their pupils when they wander off path and show what is important and what just *seems* important. If the mentor and pupil work hand in hand, the effects are profound. Therefore, seek out a trusted source within your immediate work environment and grant that person a teachable heart.

In addition to being a high producer, your mentor should be solid personally as well. Actions need to match words. The Auto Industry is pregnant with leaders that show one face at work and another after hours. As with anything, pray for guidance about accepting mentorship.

Karma Based Decisions – one of the devils greatest ploys is convincing us that karma doesn't exist.

Your actions only effect you.

You're only hurting yourself.

In the sales world we can easily succumb to the opposite as well, *the buyer will never know*, or what they don't know won't hurt them.

Years of good karma can be wiped out with this Stinkin' Thinkin'. Regardless of the dealership's view of customer service, you're accountable for your actions to a much higher power than your direct manager.

Cue karma-based decisions.

Things like disclosing vehicle issues or misleading loan terms are common temptations. We already spoke about dealing with issues head-on, but making karma-based decisions takes things a step further. Many choices force a short-term or long-term decision. Newbies make short-term and money-motivated decisions. Veterans understand that long-term decisions protect their future. When issues emerge, take a step back, weigh options, and protect the future.

In closing, it takes years to build momentum, yet it can disappear in the blink of an eye – protect yourself, and family, by living a balanced lifestyle so when the wind picks up, and rain falls, your house holds firm rather than washing away.

"The rain fell, the flood came, and the winds beat against that house, but it did not collapse because it had been founded on rock."
Matt 7:25

Chapter *Six*

Building the Customer Base

The dealership's customer base is people who have done parts, service, or sales business with the dealership and the salesperson's customer base are the prospects they personally sold. Take notice the apostrophe in dealership's and salesperson's, both indicating ownership of said customer base.

Sounds like a future conflict, doesn't it?

Both parties claim ownership and if the salesperson leaves there will no doubt be a heated discussion as to who owns the rights to their information. An earful of lawyer mumbo jumbo results in a headache and technical terms identifying the dealer as the rightful owner, but is it?

Salespeople, consider customer information theirs because they did most of the work, even prospecting outside of dealership hours and the dealership considers everyone's sales theirs because they advertise, own the inventory, and supply the roof.

157

Both are wrong. *Huh?* Really?

The customer picks whom they do business with, therefore neither "owns" them and most of the time they stick with their salesperson. *Oh, Okay.* The dealership can yell until their eyes mushroom and stomp around until their favorite loafers need another coat of shine – and may be right, but what if – *gasp* – the customer insists on buying from whom they want to?
<scratching head>
Welcome to sales court, please rise, the Honorable John P. Customer residing.

What's the big deal anyway? Who cares? *Lean forward and listen up, Champ.* There're a few important factors at play. First, future deals close easier and at higher profit margins. Secondly, they didn't cost advertising dollars. Lastly, and most importantly, returning customers are pleasant to deal with.

Build the honeycomb in three distinct ways:
- ❖ Repeat
- ❖ Referral
- ❖ Prospecting

Think babysitter. What is the process for finding one? Do we throw a dart at the phone book and trust whoever shows up? *Pffft!* Hardly! First, we call the regular sitter (repeat), and if he or she is busy, we contact friends and family to see whom they use (referral). Car buyers use this exact same process. When Kiah needs a vehicle, she returns to a trusted source or talks to friends and family to see who they recommend.

Our goal is to be the first or second option in this process: Repeat or referral.

Repeat Sales – our mission, if you so choose to accept it, is to sell a prospect *all* their future vehicles. Budget shoppers drive home in a budget vehicle today but we want another chance when more funds are available. Credit challenged buyers swallow high interest rates today, but we want them back when credit improves. New car buyers enjoy the new models and when that snazzy upgrade surfaces, we want them coming back to lick our plate clean.
Cue awkward visual.

> *"It's easy to sell **one** vehicle but takes skill to sell a customer **all** of his or her vehicles."*

It's easy to sell one vehicle, isn't it? *Think about it.* Just tell them whatever they want to hear. *Sure,* we'll warranty it until 200k miles. *Yes Sir,* this vehicle gets 50 mpg. Wave the magic discount wand and reduce the price to $4,000 under market value. *Hey bud,* lemmie see that appraisal. <adding digit to end> Dis sellin' cars stuff is damn easy, boss – when's lunch?

Achieving the first sale isn't all that impressive if you're not concerned about the future but it's quite different when the goal is to keep selling vehicles, ask for referrals, or ~~sleep at night~~ pay the light bill – *that* takes skill.

"He shall be like a tree planted by the rivers of water, that brings forth fruit in its season."
Psalms 1:3

This verse speaks about producing fruits when our actions reflect God's will. In sales, character is revealed and customers notice, which leads to multiplying fruit through future sales.

Customers long to have a trusted source. Again, think babysitter. Are you willing to pay a more for the right one? Sure. Not a lot more – but a little more is just fine. In addition, this little extra comes with expectations, right? Little Shelly's pigtails still need to be plural, Roxy's fish should be a swimmer – not a floater, and Rodney better not set fire to anything (especially near his lips). Likewise, customers give salespeople expectations.

They'd better take care of me.

Wise salespeople begin with this reciprocation cycle in mind – they make it known that they want to earn future business, and finally, they follow words with action.

The closing rate for repeat and referral buyers doubles the normal rate, which means it only takes half the leads to sell the same number of units (raises eyebrows). Avoiding the haystack search and plucking out easier sales **drastically** improves productivity. Newbies spend the majority of their day perched next to a window yelping like milk-swelled kittens waiting for traffic – or chasing down leads that are *in the wind.*

Veterans, who value their repeat buyers, just need to answer the phone and stay ~~awake waiting for finance~~ organized. Interestingly, everyone leaves satisfied, rather than puffy crossed-armed customers.

So how do we get to this level of autopilot?
Momentum.

Good to Great, by Jim Collins captures momentum perfectly with his flywheel analogy.

Look at momentum as a 10,000-pound wheel hanging on the wall and it takes every ounce of your effort to move it one inch. After pushing an entire day, the massive wheel only completes one revolution, ambitious hands keep pushing week after week and it starts getting a little easier. Months of pushing gets that wheel to make more revolutions, and after years it becomes a magnificent thing, carrying so much momentum that it cannot be stopped – it doesn't require the constant pushing it once did. Impressed onlookers see this massive spinning wheel, yet have no idea of what it took to create its force.

Salesperson's struggle = the 10,000-pound wheel.

Many push the wheel, get discouraged, and search for an easier wheel – momentum's fruits never happen because salespeople neglect their Customer Base.

The average trade cycle is 24-30 months, meaning from the purchase date to the time upgraded. Interestingly, most buyers don't even know they have a trade cycle. "We plan to keep it forever!" The thrilled buyer says during delivery. Throughout the next two years, the joy of new eventually wears off – squished by little fingers sporting Sippy cups and French fries, or stroke-worthy repair estimates.

Trust the numbers.

Even if the customer isn't showing signs of trading raise your antenna around the 18-month mark and get ahead of this naturally reoccurring cycle.

Use this sold-owner follow-up process to push your wheel
- ✓ 1 day after sale – Send a thank you card with a personal note inside.
- ✓ 7 days after sale – Welcome them back to review options, or answer any questions. The joy of new is strong. Referral hunt!
- ✓ 30 days after sale - Ensure the vehicle meets needs: Fuel mileage, seating, or work needs, if not, discuss trade-in possibilities (rare).
- ✓ 90 days after sale – Set First Service Appointment, and inform about service specials.
- ✓ Contact even 6 months – Figure out trade cycle of all household vehicles.
- ✓ Happy Anniversary Card (one year after purchase).
- ✓ Happy Birthday Card – buyer and spouse.
- ✓ Add customer to newsletter circulation.

Throughout the process, aim to understand all the household needs. If Uncle Scott just treated himself to a flashy Ford truck, then figure out when Aunt Nadine plans to replace her current vehicle. Hey, what about the kids? *Yup.* Chase down those squirts too and understand the new drivers and figure out how to get them on board – full-service, my friend.

Adam, one of the best salespeople I've ~~competed~~ worked with, took a step further and scheduled service appointments. He picked up vehicles at workplaces and dropped it back off when finished. Furthermore, he knew when Little Johnny pitched his first little league game and had a Dairy Queen gift certificate waiting in the mailbox congratulating him afterwards. *Cue Clap Track.*

Will Adam sell more vehicles to that household?
Um, yeah.

Referral Sales – are prospects recommended by an outside source such as friends, family, unsold prospects, or sold customers. Casey sells a vehicle to Gloria and she sends in her buddy, Jeffrey. Referrals are rewarding – it's the ultimate level of trust, isn't it? Trusting someone is one thing, but it's another matter to send others. This gesture certainly carries an indirect message: I am willing risk my word that you will take care of Jeffrey.

Walk-Ins stalk the lot and grumble: "Just looking." Referrals stalk up to the nearest salesperson and demand to work with only one person – *you* – and they're never just looking.

"Hi there." Says Jeffrey. "Gloria sent me down here to work with you. I need help finding ~~training wheels for my Harley~~ a new Ford truck."

"Great. Nice to meet you. I'm going to be tied up for another hour selling this Fusion, would you like to work with someone else, or wait?"

"No, I'm only working with you. I'll see you after lunch."

We make more money off these buyers? *Huh?* Not a typo. Before picking up thou lashing stick – please allow me to explain.

First, loyal customers allow you make a little money off them – *just not too much*. In fact, they often insist, or at least confirm, "You made a little money, right? Good, I wanna make sure that you're taken care of." Second, they are worried about being taken to the cleaner, and avoid this threat by dealing with a trusted source. Third, they haven't price shopped every dealer within a two-hour radius – yes, they may keep you honest by getting a competitor's price, but allow you to match or beat it – and this scenario almost always results in higher profit margins. Lastly, the appraiser's pen creates additional profit. If he or she knows the vehicle, they put more money into it, which equals higher gross.

Referrals are the very definition of multiplying fruit. First, we basket fruit from the original deal, which bears more fruit through additional referrals, those people recommend more, and on and on it goes. Therefore, deem every customer as a new branch. Each branch has potential to sprout more branches and the number of branches determines the trunks health. View every sold customer as an account manager; much like a tree branch "manages" the stems growing from it. This attitude helps keep the branch, and tree, healthy.

If Elijah buys a vehicle and refers Jacob, shouldn't I treat Jacob's potential issues as if Elijah's future deals depend on it as well? They all tie together. Therefore, treat Elijah as the head of that branch, or account.

164

One of my favorite branches began as a very tough customer, named Petar. He lashed me with his homemade whip while buying a new Ford dually diesel truck. *Charming.* Behaving much like other high credit score buyers, he lined up hot coals and ran me back and forth with an eyebrow raised. Three attempts at closing him all failed, and I grew frustrated (mucho mucho). This went on for over three weeks.

Cue common ground hunt.

Oh, you manage a race team? *Perfect.* Friday night I stood outside his pit box with a smile that touched both my ears and matching mechanics gloves.

Monday, we got our sale.

A couple days later, his first referral wandered in. Those referrals referred others. Within two years, this branch bore 20 sales. What happens when Monday morning rolls around and there is a distraught message from one of Petar's referrals? We treat everyone well, but a great big light blinks between my ears, warning me to be careful not to saw that branch off my tree.

What is the best way to ask for referrals? IT'S NOT, "Do you know anyone looking for a vehicle?" Even though statistics say that one out of three people know someone looking for a vehicle, there is a better way.

"Out of your friends, family, or coworkers who is next to purchase a vehicle?"

This phrase always draws an answer. If Mom just purchased then its Dad's turn next – it's always *someone's* turn even if they aren't looking right now. Then follow with:

"Would they be ready in the next few days, weeks, or months?

Develop a timeline, and assess their needs. *Cue registration form.* Now you have a timeline and a good picture of needs – let's create a little urgency, shall we?

"If I run across a really nice trade that fits your needs can I call you, or just let it go?"

Sheesh! Ya better grab a bigger basket, Bud. That little old thing will never hold all the fruit from this method. The sale won't be immediate but certainly within reach. How many leads stack up before you're hawking every new trade coming in? Heck, folks don't even have their trade cleaned out and the high producers dart up, sniff its tailpipe, and rush off to find it a new mate.

Setting deals up before they hit the lot is a great way to sell – they are owned right, and provide something no other dealer can give: Background. Trades have a story and prospects love buying vehicles that they know the background on.
<nose in the air>
Smell that, Champ? Yup. Higher gross.

Bird Dog – Some ~~jerks~~ states don't allow salespeople to pay for referrals – dubbed, bird dog. They also don't allow speeding, jaywalking, or swearing after whacking your thumb with a hammer (wink wink).

In addition, not all dealers have referral programs. Regardless of stuffy attitudes, resourceful salespeople can figure out a way to incentivize others. *Others? Huh? Don't you mean customers?* Sure, customers give the best referrals but you can incentivize *anyone* to give leads:

- ✓ Parts Store Clerks
- ✓ Farmers
- ✓ Mechanics
- ✓ Camp Ground Staff
- ✓ Tow Truck Drivers
- ✓ Quick Lube Advisors
- ✓ Salvage Yard Employees
- ✓ Tire Shop Advisors
- ✓ Driver Ed instructors
- ✓ New Auburn Goat Herders
- ✓ Poskin's Proud Pet Petters

Gift certificates, free detail, dinner for two, or gas cards make great non-cash incentives. Interestingly, my best referral source refused to accept compensation – he wanted the referrals taken care of and that was payment enough.

Petar never took a nickel.

Prospecting sales – are sales driven from outside the dealership. *Oh, great.* Here we go – you want me to tug shirts at family reunions? *Good grief,* no. Hang in there, kid. There are much better ways.

<u>Three prospecting Tactics:</u>

- ✓ The Expert Within the Circle
- ✓ Indirect
- ✓ Direct

Effective prospecting is a key piece of a high producer's pie. As stated, half of your sales should come from your own efforts (repeat, referral, and prospecting). Lot-dependent salespeople are inconsistent. One month they eat chicken and the next month only the feathers – prospecting stabilizes results immensely.

Many people dread prospecting because they don't like imposing on people. *Be gone, Pushy Salesperson! And take your whistle with ya!*

Expert with the circle – is the most effective form of prospecting. And the best part: Zero shirt tuggin'.

Buyers seek you out.

People like to buy from whom they know – especially on large purchases. If your sister in law sold houses and you're in the market, then surely, she gets a call. What if no friends or family sold houses? *Hmmm.* Well, we'd pluck someone out of our circles.
Doesn't Casey, from hockey, sell houses?
I'll talk to her Thursday at practice.

Most people don't know someone who sells cars, therefore eliminating the first two choices. Knowing this, get involved in many circles thus making yourself available as a go-to person. Producing sales is surprising simple.

→ Join circle.
→ Become active within the circle.
→ Talk about your profession – things that are not common knowledge.
→ Become known as the "car guy', or expert.
→ Keep attending functions.
→ Refraineth from drinketh too much wineth.
→ Bring a pen to write down leads. It's that easy.

Some leads come from within the circle but *most* come from someone the group member knows.
Did a light bulb just flicker on?

168

Even a small group is amplified to an astounding number of potential sales. Little Marley's flag footballs team only has 20 team members, which equates to around 40 parents. Because most of leads come front someone the parents know, not from the parents themselves, we cannot look at Marley's flag football as 40 potential people. *Tipping Point*, by Malcolm Gladwell states that humans can effectively nurture 200 relationships; therefore, Marely's flag football represents a net that covers 8,000 people.

This is just one circle.

Increasing the number of circles creates a staggering amount of people. An aggressive salesperson could easily handle three, four, or five circles. We just jumped our net to cover 20,000 to 40,000 people. How many members does your church carry? Hundreds? *And no*, I'm not advocating to hand business cards down the pew but your profession will come up. Through consistent contact, character is revealed, leading to people wanting to do business, or recommend, someone they know and trust.

Dumb question: *How much does this little activity cost?* Need a hint? It rhymes with HERO:

ZERO.

Beyond the gas and the time investment, we create sales by doing little more than showing up.

My most productive circle started with that invite to the racetrack. Friday nights, I found myself in a new circle of about 15 people and got introduced to new people each week – increasing the circle. Within a few weeks, people sought me out and asked about new trucks and diesel information – care to guess what I started driving to the track? *Yuppers*, new trucks. We sold a few vehicles.

Cue bigger investment.

Service department, I have an idea. Make us up one of dem der pace trucks. They lowered an F150, put wide big-lettered tires on it, and wrapped it in an American flag – installing "In God We Trust' on the rear window. Price tag: $5,000. *Sheesh!* This better work, kid. *Cue work shirt.* Anxieties quickly dissolved after selling more cars – in fact, over two years, I traced back over $50,000 in profits to the leads gathered on Friday night. In addition, we sold that custom truck without losing a nickel. As a bonus, the track allowed quests to ride-along inside the pace truck.

Sounds like a great way to reward future referrals, doesn't it? Many non-cash bird dogs were delighted to climb in the pace truck and lead rumbling cars around the track.

This turned out to be a great bonus to something I was already doing – it wasn't as easy as it sounds – after all – I did have to carry a pen, wear a work shirt, and keep mustard off my chin.

Consistent presence within the circle is key. My racing circle met every Friday night and other circles like hockey met multiple times per week. Get involved in things that meet on a consistent basis and that you enjoy so you look forward to doing it. For those struggling to live a balanced lifestyle, bring the kids along.

Ideas for circles:

- ❖ Chamber of commerce
- ❖ Horse Shows
- ❖ Masons
- ❖ Cattle Shows
- ❖ Churches
- ❖ Fatherhood Programs
- ❖ Farm Bureau
- ❖ FFA
- ❖ At-Risk Kids Programs
- ❖ Little League
- ❖ Race Tracks
- ❖ Flag Football
- ❖ Hockey

Indirect Prospecting — requires setting up a presence within an event and displaying products. We still avoid tugging on shirtsleeves (yay!). The sale doesn't happen at the event but later on after the dust settles. Hand out items throughout the event, simple things such as bottled water on a hot day is effective, or anything with our contact information. Gather information and identify people within trade cycles – *wait for it* – and then figure out how to sell them products.

Ideas for indirect prospecting:

- ❖ County Fairs
- ❖ Festivals
- ❖ Carnivals
- ❖ Meets
- ❖ Horse Shows
- ❖ Events
- ❖ Rodeos
- ❖ Gun Shows
- ❖ Charlie Manson's Parole Hearings

Those working with larger budgets can offer prize drawings. Display a prize and have contestants' fill out contact information to qualify. "Winners will be notified by email", is a good way to get valid email addresses for future marketing. Include a box for how long they have owned their current vehicle – anyone over 24 months is low hanging fruit for trading. Set up in high traffic areas and it won't require staffing. Return to the location periodically to retrieve entries and start plucking the low hanging fruit through calling entries. Sales offset the cost of the giveaway. To increase response rates, legitimize the giveaways by taking pictures of past winners and display them near the giveaway.

Direct Prospecting – ok, ya little shirt tuggers – you're going in. Brush your ~~tooth~~ teeth and grab your best smile, it's time to ~~pay the bookie~~ go to work.

This form of prospecting directly engages people. Even though God blessed salespeople with the gift of gab, we grumble about approaching cold contacts without a reason. *So make a reason!*

Identify a problem and then specialize in fixing that problem. Products have multiple uses, right? Groups have specialized needs.   Be resourceful, consider your target group's needs and then tailor opening lines to meet those needs. *Oh, ok.* This wedges a foot in the door and lets you build the sale.

- ❖ Fleet accounts: "We specialize in businesses that are large enough to seek a heavy discount and free pickup and drop off."

- ❖ Horse Owners: "We specialize in ~~proving you're loaded~~ super duty trucks and accessories."

❖ Government Vehicle Grant Programs: "We specialize in providing vehicles that meet year, miles, price, and condition requirements."

❖ Government Officials: "We specialize in providing worry-free seating – capable of producing 6-8 hours of paid sleep." *Oops, my bad.*

My favorite cold prospecting method was driving trucks to campgrounds and approaching any vehicle that had no business getting hooked up to a large camper. Dodge Durango's and Ford Explorers might have V8 engines but the rear suspensions don't support large pull behind campers, especially when loaded down with gear. Definitely, steer clear from these contraptions heading north at 70 mph. *Yikes.*

But hey, why not pull up to a campsite and talk trucks?

They already drive vehicles that are hard on the fuel budget (V8 SUV has same mpg as a truck) – upgrading to trucks makes sense.

"We specialize in keeping that good-looking camper away from Oak Trees, pedestrians, and your rear hatch." Hotdogs won't be the only thing you leave campsites with.

Festive mood + Good sales cheer = L.E.A.D.S
<superhero cape flaps in the wind>

Again, hawk trade cycles – and not just our existing customers. A little light bulb should flicker on anytime a person has owned their vehicle longer than 24 months. Existing customers, prospecting leads, or complete strangers are all low hanging fruit to the salesperson that asks. "How long have owned your vehicle?" Trust the stats – assume people that have owned their vehicle longer than two years may be sick of their ride. Push them over the edge by giving them a reason to trade.

"The Dahlberg's son Rodney is looking for a Dodge Power Wagon, just like yours, he won't take anything that's been smoked in and I know you guys took good care of it. I could probably get you a couple extra bucks if you're willing to trade it in."

Assuming you're tending your field, there should be a handful of prospects you are on the lookout for. *Cue high producers*. They produce more with less leads because they constantly reach back into their memory banks and pull out specific people that MIGHT be interested in their prospects trade. Do we really care if Rodney buys the trade? *Nope*, not really. Two sales are better than one but creating urgency on the current deal is the goal.

Sales Tool – Carpenters hammer mortgage payments away one thump at a time. Nurses squeeze away bills one cuff at a time. And salespeople earn commission with a handy dandy pen. This is the mark of a committed salesperson – one that has fully bought in: He or she *always* carries a pen.

"Hey. I got a buddy that is looking for a vehicle. Can you help?"

"Sure, what is his number?"

Always be prepared for this common situation.

174

In closing, Our Creator gave us a great example to live by – Jesus came and lived as a servant to us all.

> *"If I then, your Lord and Teacher, have washed your feet, you also ought to wash one another's feet."*
> **John 13:14**

This verse speaks to serving one another whether there is a reward involved or not. Serve your customer base – be attentive to needs and complete tasks with a thankful heart. Salespeople are blessed to have a career in which they can follow this example and make a great living at the same time.

The Auto Sales Industry struggles to employ people with good character; therefore, it's easy to stand out.

Prediction: Combine character with these tips and your customer base will grow at an astounding rate – helping to build momentum and achieve autopilot years earlier. Life on the showroom floor is completely different once a salesperson is no longer lot-dependent and creates his or her sales through the techniques described in this chapter.

Chapter *Seven*

Harmony
A pleasing arrangement of parts.

Think of environments that spark a reaction within your heart. *Can you label it?* These feelings surround us all the time. At home, it surfaces with our spouse's anger – two steps inside the door and negative energy smacks you in the face like a shovel (97% chance that I earned it). Perhaps, your child stomps of the buss and fills the house with the day's frustrations. We *feel* something amiss.

How about the opposite?
Can you feel a concert's electricity?
The crowd engulfs you like a tidal wave – rippling energy throughout.
What about church's serenity?
Do you feel God's Spirit drawing you near?
Again, energy *felt* – not seen.

The dealership strives to stir up good emotions as well. Creating and preserving good atmosphere is one of the team's greatest functions – and not easy. We accomplish buzz through teamwork *and* individual effort. Working together, being customer focused, using process, and adopting correct attitudes are cultures key ingredients.

Hey, wait a minute. Aren't these things out of a salesperson's control? Agreed, *some* of these things are out of the salesperson's hands – after all, managers build culture and salespeople operate within it, but understanding that unseen energy is a major factor for both parties. A salesperson's value is measured in many ways – don't assume that selling product is the most important factor.

Surely, outselling others will secure my seat at the table?

Better check your math on that one, bud. Even if you can sell hair to a barber – if you hurt harmony – out ya go. *Gulp.* Team dynamics are just too important and leadership wisely protects it.

Selling is easy. Financing is easy. Repairing is easy. Detailing is easy. Selling parts is easy. Getting everyone to work together in a pleasing arrangement is a different matter entirely. *Ugh. Sure is.* Each department could stand alone, sales would still sell vehicles, service would still repair vehicles, and parts could still sell parts without the other departments present but *all* would do less business – much less. Each department feeds the others, making each perform better.

Harmony is the world's great equalizer. A dealership with good harmony runs circles around bigger stores. And the best part: *It's free.* Thousands of advertising dollars and abundant inventory doesn't produce sales or happy customers – flop down obscene wages and dealerships still sputters around the production track. In contrast, if a dealership sets up conditions in a pleasing arrangement, they enjoy high production regardless of conditions. Call it many things: Humorous, entertaining, karmas wheel, or perhaps part of His divine plan – *but make no mistake* – harmony's effect is a game changer and one that levels the playing field.

How do we get departments working together and what specific points can you do to make the system operate better? Let's review areas to make a *pleasing* impact.

Personality Gifts – Our first step on harmony's ship is adjusting expectations. Children indulge in a term called Magical Thinking whereas they assume the whole world revolves around them rather than the sun. In addition, they assume that others think just like they do and process information the same. Eventually, pampers are tossed aside yet much Stinkin' Thinkin' lingers into adulthood.

<opening the window>

Each department needs a certain personality type to function well. Our Creator installed different gifts in each one of us (It's true, I checked Corinthians myself). Each personality gift compliments the others, thus creating a better whole.

Think diet plus exercise.

Dieting helps Casey lose five pounds. Exercise helps Russell lose five pounds. Nathan combines diet and exercise and loses 20 pounds. Combining personality gifts produces an outcome that each element couldn't do on its own.

"Be in the same mind toward one another.
Don't set your mind on high things,
but associate with the humble.
Don't be wise in your own opinion."
Romans 12:16

Read between the lines. *What is the indirect message?* Be humble and accept other personality types – *especially* the drastic differences across departments. Avoid judging others and be grateful that specific needs are covered, which through synergy, helps your department produce more.

The dealership cannot fill every department with sales personalities, which buy the way, would be a disaster. *Clean up isle five!*

"Having gifts differ according to the grace given to us, let us use them."
Romans 12:6

Just like appreciating preachers for their ability to preach, appreciate Service Techs for their ability to repair; Finance Managers for their ability to structure deals; and Parts Managers for their inventory management skills. Each position requires a different personality type, and rather than being critical about what others lack in sales skills, appreciate the things they are better at, and be grateful those positions help you sell more vehicles – albeit, indirectly.

This dynamic is lost on households every day. Spouses are critical to their mate for being weak outside their role and discount their strengths. This creates a cycle of undesired side effects that kills peace.

"Hunt for things that your spouse does better than you, and there, you'll find peace."
- C.J. Penn

Let's bounce off a few key cats – explain their importance, and give some tips to feed harmony.

Finance Manager – is a heavy hitter on the sales floor. They input, submit, and work deals with lenders – *everyone's* deals. Dealerships don't overstock this position and they handle a mountain of work. Finance Managers have many paychecks sitting on their desk, implying if terms aren't figured out then no one gets paid. Those who take that responsibility seriously don't have time for small talk and might even neglect updating you on the status of your deal. Help this position by turning in complete, legible paperwork, ask who updates the customer (you or them). Stay away from small talk, especially when busy and don't get offended if missing paperwork sparks this dog barking.
Finance Managers don't like salespeople present while they present finance menus so disappear when they come out, yet stay close enough to slide back in while waiting for paperwork to be completed.

Prime your customers to be open-minded about back-end products. Not every customer benefits from gap, warranty, credit life, and disability but many do. If the buyer lives paycheck to paycheck, these products protect more than the vehicle. What happens when a person must pick between making a loan payment or a vehicle repair? Getting to work trumps the bank, thus risking credit – these products hedge against those very risks. Finance Managers don't want salespeople pitching back-end products, but priming customers to be open helps immensely.

Detailers – deal with a never-ending stack of work and sales, service, and parts department constantly pull them away from doing their actual job. Most detailers accept this as a way of life, yet others get testy about this constant redirection, so keep this in mind when making requests.

Most detailers take pride in their work so be mindful of that when using vehicles for non-sales related activity – instead, grab dirty vehicles. This helps keep the inventory looking good and helps the detail department stay productive by working on fresh trades rather than redoing work.

Wearing sleeves, Champ?

Great, roll them up. Wash vehicles for appointments rather than throwing the keys and demanding vehicles be ready by a certain time. Detailers notice and reciprocate by helping when you're in a pinch. Washing vehicles only takes five minutes and is time well spent. Get instruction about which bays to use and then clean up when finished.

I see ya smashing all that coffee... why not use it on something more productive rather than Candy Crush?

In addition, provide feedback about vehicle conditions. Inform the head detailer about touch ups or items missed during the initial detail. Even if he or she didn't do the work let them correct team members rather than you. Refrain from nitpicking, but things to their attention that would hinder a sale.

Some shops have a process for vehicle get-ready's and expect it to be followed, and some don't – figuring this out is a giant step in keeping harmony. If they have a process then use it. If not, run things through the head detailer and let them delegate the work. Furthermore, give advance notice whenever possible. "This vehicle needs to be done ASAP.", isn't respectful and rarely creates friends. Find middle ground by giving advance notice.

In closing. sparkle a detailer's eye by recognizing their work. "Hey, you did a great job on that vehicle, it looks so much better now. You really increased the value of this one. I love working with you." Things like this, spoken with a sincere heart, fuel the tank of a position that typically doesn't see big paychecks.

Service Writer – is a swing position, meaning they must understand how clocks are built and communicate time clearly. On one side they have a row full of techs to delegate work to (not known for their people skills), and the other side is lined up with cross-armed customers.

Service Writers shine
by delivering gritty messages in a clean way.

Service Writers constantly walk the line between creating shop revenue yet keeping bills manageable – preserving trust throughout. Safety items cannot be taken lightly and failing to catch issues are a constant threat. Think family doctor. They deal with these same factors. They must communicate bad news in a tactful way yet push urgency with neglected issues.

"Little Caleb swallowed a quarter, what should we do?" *Hmmm.* Wait for him to dispense an item, or demand a refund?

Much like a Finance Manager, Service Writers have loaded plates. They're busy early in the morning, again at lunch, and before going home – avoid small talk during these times, but DO connect during other times because they are a valuable source of information and leads. Build rapport with Service Writers the same you would with customers: Common ground and teaming up. Service Writers are the first to know when estimates are declined, which is an opportunity for a resourceful salesperson. Surely, a person that refuses a large estimate might consider trading and just like anyone else giving referrals, a Service Writers won't give leads to just anyone – so prove your worthy.

~~Ba ba ba Bird Dog!~~

Service Techs – these cats have a set of instructions installed at birth that give them an amazing ability to figure out problems. Sometimes they know how to fix problems before they start, and other times figure it out as they go. Tough repairs are met with a person resourceful enough to figure it out. They consult other techs or manuals if needed. Resourcefulness is a way of life.

Communication isn't a strong point.

There, I said it, and I'm not taking it back.

Complaint Process: Secure favorite crayon, jot down gripe, lick the envelope and send to Raised-By-Mechanics-And-Understand-Them Blvd.

Their gifts rest at the opposite end of the spectrum as salespeople – and by no means implying that one is more important. After all, no one tells time without the clock builder – simply pointing out that these two personality types are bound to have friction. *And they do...* Avoid this friction by speaking to the Service Writer instead, and stay out of the tech's way.

But why? Maybe my extra special communication skills would win them over?

Techs are paid flat rate, meaning if the book calls for one 1.2 hours and the repair takes 2.5 hours — they only get paid for 1.2, respect this by not eating into their pocketbook with small talk. Besides that, techs throw darts at salespeople's photos during lunch so getting close enough to receive a puncture wound is a bad idea.

If brave enough to try building rapport with this group, start by asking the technical details about specific vehicles and then engage your ears. Truck information is fruitful because truck buyers like hearing feedback where the rubber hits the road, meaning the people who work on them – fancy brochures don't hold a candle to information coming from people who spend days washing their hands from manufacture's mistakes. Stick to fact-finding missions before work, during lunch, or after work – most techs get to the dealership before salespeople but leave earlier so hit them up on their way out.

Author herby relinquishes all responsibility for black eyes, missing teeth, or darts sticking out of salesperson's bottom.

Understanding each position props up harmony within the store, you cannot do much about how others interact but you can control how you respond. For instance, if a coworker just threw keys at a detailer and demanded his or her vehicle be ready in 20 minutes and you unknowingly walk up and need something done, don't be offended about getting a cold shoulder. I've found this exact scenario to be

184

in play throughout the dealership – a *magical-thinking* Salesperson creates friction and frustrations are rubbed off on the next person in line. *Lovely.*

Sales Managers – let's cover the most important relationships a salesperson has to master: The Sales Manager and Desk Manager. A desker provides numbers for the salesperson to present to customers and structures deals for finance. A Sales Manager runs the sales floor. They train, make sure salespeople complete sold and unsold follow up, and help close customers.

Some dealerships separate this position and others combine it.

This relationship is crucial.

Your ability to communicate effectively with him or her is vital to ~~sanity~~ harmony and determines the quality of your workday. Every manager operates the sales floor differently, and if multiple managers control the same area, it complicates things.
Think parents.
Each has a different role and rules. *How did you handle this as a child?* Surely, you ~~conned~~ navigated Mom different from Dad. The same theory applies here; treat the Floor Manager as Mom, and the Desker as Dad and *NEVER* assume that everyone is on the same page. Often, one manager wants things a certain way and the other will be completely different, so don't let it upset you, expect it – and then operate specifically to each managers expectation. Conflicting expectations means getting the Desker and Floor Manager together to clarify.

Best of luck, Champ.

Sound like a pain?
Yup, it is. So are new salespeople: Y*ou're even.*

Proper T.O – This means Turning Over a customer to someone else. The auto industry has a high failure rate and our answer is to put a second set of ears in motion whenever possible – especially when new salespeople are involved. Get a manager involved anytime you fail at getting to the next step on the Road to the Sale, and definitely, before a customer ~~bolts~~ leaves.

"Without counsel, plans go awry, but in the multitude of counselors they are established."
Proverbs 15:22

Many salespeople struggle because they refuse to open their hearts to instruction and insist on doing things their way. METAPHOR ALERT!

Jeffrey gathers his fishing gear and heads to Bass Lake. He's never fished before, but how hard can it be? He loads his hook, steps to the bank, and swings the pole to cast his line. The bobber barely makes it past his feet and the line goes everywhere. *Yikes!* After some wrestling, the tangled line gets bigger and ends up in a balled mess. Upset, Jeffrey sits on a rock and contemplates what to do.

186

Fishing looks so easy, what happened?

Before long, Pete an experienced fisherman, strolls over and asks if he needs help. Jeff gladly hands his pole over and Pete starts untangling the line but grows frustrated because Jeffrey's hands are bumping into his, making it difficult to fix. In the end, Pete reaches over, snips the line, and starts over with a fresh hook, line, and bobber.

When it comes to accepting help – *wait for it* – salespeople are just like Jeffrey and not willing to completely hand over their tangled mess. A manager evaluates the situation and determines whether to untangle the line or start new (new needs assessment), either way, it's impossible with a second set off hands in the way. Avoid this by falling back whenever a manager interacts with customers – and engage learning mode.

Veterans also get prideful in this situation. They have plenty of opportunities to T.O. – yet reject it. Sounds like a star basketball player who refuses to pass, doesn't it? Sure, the star is good, but if actions hurt the overall team, isn't that a problem? Regardless of skill level, accept help and raise your closing percentage.

Times to T.O.
- ✓ Failure to get to the next step on the Road to the Sale
- ✓ Unable to get on the Road to the Sale
- ✓ Overly technical customers
- ✓ Unable to get over a negative
- ✓ Getting ran over
- ✓ Before the customer leaves
- ✓ Getting beat over the head and neck area with Gina's Cadillac-sized purse.

If the store's goals aren't met, the manager gets axed rather than the salespeople. *Cue training, follow up, and getting involved.* Single deal in house + newbie salesperson = managers full attention.

Whether help is requested or not.

If this happens, resist slipping into offended mode and put on your learning ears instead. And just like a T.O., give over total control.

Healthy communication is key when building trust with the Desker. Again, compare this to parent-child relationship. Parents don't need every little detail about a school trip (sale), but shouldn't be left in the dark about important issues. Specifically, update the Desker on stalled deals, negative feedback on vehicles, upset customers, after-sale issues, stalled service issues, and leaving the store just to name a few. Resist the urge to barrage the Desker with every little detail but make significant details known.

Deskers focus on worksheets and they know that one worksheet represents a pile of eggs that never hatched. In fact, worksheets take priority over almost everything else (with the exception of masked gunman looking to steal my wife). If your worksheet is the priority, great – but if not, resist growing impatient and wait to handle your issue alter the dust settles.

In addition, get clear expectations. How are worksheets presented? How are commitments handled? Deskers are sensitive about worksheets. After learning the Road to the Sale, sit next to the Desker and watch how they interact with others. Learn by watching others.

Avoid loose ends. It's better to discount the price than have a list of hanging items after the sale. Most of the time, issues are not deal breakers – customers simply see how far they can push a salesperson.

New salespeople = get ran over.
Veterans = discount instead of making promises.

Be black and white regarding items promised and inform the Desker right away. They are responsible for holding gross and keeping volume high. Accepting a zero profit deal is tolerable but going into the red isn't – avoid surprises by informing about issues right away so the Desker can make educated decisions.

Don't ask about profit on a working deal. *Cue bad etiquette.* Managers look out for the long-term interests of the store and profits reflect that, sometimes profit hangs over the beltline and other times it's wearing skinny jeans – being critical about profit is like a six-year-old blowing a whistle at an orchestra. Most manager's pay plans are heavily based from gross.

Translation: What's good for you, is good for them.

Furthermore, there are behind-the-scenes factors that heavily influence the final price. Often, customers agree to pay more than lenders will finance. Thus, creating an interesting dynamic – either the customer has to put money down, or the Desker must reduce price. Accepting smaller profit wrinkles a salesperson's nose, but volume is in the best interest of the store so trust your Desker and don't criticize.

Let's move on.

Process – is harmony's magic potion. Processes bring good fruit such as, higher volume, better quality control, and controlling customers. Each step during the Road to the Sale brings us closer to making the sale and avoids threats, which results in higher sales volume. It also ensures that we don't excluded important things such as, needs assessment, walk around, and trial closing. This reduces the risk of customers leaving with products that don't fit needs, which hurts the dealership and salesperson's reputation.

Almost all dealerships have processes, but rarely write them down, thus making it difficult to find rhythm – especially when new. *No sweat, my pet*. Do it yourself. Write down key processes and then lean on those notes until you have them down by heart. Keep each process to five or six steps. There is a process sheet in the back of this book, simply make a copy and get with a manager or fellow salesperson and write down your dealership's specific steps.

A sample sheet might look like this:
1. **Pulling Credit**: Signed form → log into Dealertrack → input info → submit → find in archives staple printout to registration form

2. **New Trade in:** New key tag → add new stock number → park in fresh trade row → give keys to service

3. **Delivery:** Wash vehicle → add business cards in manual (sales and service writer) complete service walk → match radio presets to trade → review options

4. **Locating Keys:** Check board → check vehicle → check service → check detail → check appraisal desk → slam head between two large objects

Your board might look completely different. This helps reap the rewards of the process itself, but also helps become less of a burden on others by being self-sufficient.

The Buddy System – is when two salespeople make an agreement to help each other. Dealerships split sales schedules into morning (7:30 a.m. - 5 p.m.), and night (10 a.m.-8 pm) shifts which leaves a gap in coverage. If Kobe's customer comes in and Kobe is gone, the staff knows that Jamaar is Kobe's buddy on the Buddy System and turns the customer over to Jamaar.

Kill two birds with one stone: Sell more vehicles *and* foster harmony. Kobe fills Jamaar in on customer details when he leaves, which is a smoother transition for returning customers. Without the buddy system, returning customers have to repeat themselves, which hurts rapport and discounts the customer's experience.

Some buddy systems split commission on shared deals, and others don't – the salespeople work out the arrangement between each other. A well-balanced salesperson needs to spend time outside the store and can prevent losing money, or feeling guilty by using a buddy system.

Lace up those running shoes, Champ – it's time to chase down our natural enemy: *Time*

Time Kills Deals – Imagine flipping over a big hourglass with every new prospect, except we never know how much sand is inside. Running out of time highly frustrates everyone involved and with a couple tricks can be kept to a minimum.

Speeding up and slowing down is a great defensive for lighting time. *Slowing down? Huh?* Hang in there, gimmie a second to explain. *The Law of Reciprocation* states that when we receive something of value, we feel obligated to give something back.

Of value?

Whatcha talkn' bout Willis?

Traditionally, this means money but we can give other things too such as, products, time, or **effort**, which compels people to reciprocate.

Speeding up: My salesperson gives extra effort – look at him hustling to help us.

Slowing down: My salesperson gives extra time and makes sure we understand.

By constantly shifting between slowing down and speeding up, we build valuable reciprocation points and cash them in later.

My salesperson earned this sale –
I had better stay and finish.

My salesperson tried the best she can,
let's do the $239/mo. instead of $219.

192

Through speeding up and slowing down, we extend time. So yes, even slowing down defends us – by *granting* a time extension.

When to Hustle	**When to Slow Down**
Gathering trade info	Needs Assessment
Pulling up vehicles	Walk around
Washing trades	Reviewing options
Getting finance info	Worksheet
Washing deliveries	

Working hard and compelling reciprocation are very simple concepts, but, in the end, it's these simple things help us jump over complex huddles and secure the sale. Be wise and hedge against these things throughout the sale.   This should perk the ears of newbies – how much training does one need to master giving extra effort?

Um, zero.

These cats create a distinct advantage, and it costs them nothing.

Customer Complaints – are inevitable. *We sell machines!* Whether brand new or enough miles to offend the space shuttle – count on one thing: Machines fail.

Great! That means we can tell customers to beat it, right?
Yikes. No, sir.

Refrain from average dealer mode, who utters lawyer mumbo jumbo whenever problems surface.   Isn't it ~~ridiculous~~ interesting how quickly best-friend Bob turns into lawyer Bob at the first hint of an after-sale problem?

"Under state law, article three, subsection one, it clearly states that vehicles purchased as-is are no longer required to be repaired by short-term thinking dealer, therefore will not consider assisting vehicle current owner and herein relinquish any opportunity to sell future products to friends, family, coworkers, or anyone with ears."

"But Bob, I just bought it yesterday."

"Sorry we can no longer speak to you without your attorney present."

Perhaps a bit exaggerated, but this little dance is in full swing in most dealerships across the country. Don't fall into this trap. As stated earlier, problems provide an opportunity. Through problems, we show that we're different *and* prove they did business with the right place.

Will it be easy? Nope.

First, be clear on who handles complaints: The salesperson, manager, or owner? Avoid stepping on toes by using the current process. As an owner, I felt after-sale issues warranted my full attention and I insisted to be the only one to handle it, and wouldn't tolerate anyone going around me. If this is your situation. Great – it's a good sign that your store treats complaints seriously. If not, and you're the soldier holding the fire hose let us review some tips on extinguishing fires.

You too, can prevent forest fires...

If the complaint is vehicle related (well, duh), then always get the vehicle in for inspection. Send a tow truck or truck and trailer. Withhold any judgment, opinion, or attitude until after a tech inspects it, your tech.

"You don't have to attend every argument that you're invited to."
-Leandro Herrero

Simply agree to get together after the inspection. After you have all the facts, it's time for our friend Mr. Process to join us: The Blank Paper Process.

→ Grab a blank paper and Move to private area
→ Tell customer your goal
→ Write down the complaint
→ Repeat the complaint in your own words
→ Ask what they feel is fair
→ Review options with a decision maker

1. **Moving to a private** area curbs grandstanding, if outsiders are present it complicates how both parties interact – in studies, researchers coined this behavior the Hawthorn Effect. People behave differently when the camera is rolling. In fact, so inversely that it skews the tests result and reduces the quality of the data. There may not be cameras on the showroom floor but the eyes of others have the same effect. Eliminate this by moving to a secluded area.

2. **Next, tell the customer that your goal is to have him or her walk back through the door content and willing to do future business.**

3. **Have them explain the situation**. Our creator gave us two ears and only one mouth so wad up some duct tape and stuff it in thy flapper and engage listen mode, detail the points on the blank paper.

4. **Summarize what you heard**. We do this for three reasons: Venting defuses angers, helps feel understood, and attempts to uncover unknown information. If anyone else has been involved, there

is a great chance that some discrepancies need to be ~~exposed~~ shaken loose.

5. **Ask what they think is fair**. Feeling understood fosters flexibility. Furthermore, they expect to walk into the lawyer mumbo jumbo routine and are quite surprised to have a sincere person instead. Their ideas just *miiight* be better than your own.

6. **Be resourceful**. Get with decision makers and create solutions.   The two-choice method comes to mind. For cheap repairs, perhaps the customer pays for parts if the dealer installs them. For dealer error – meaning a botched inspection – perhaps service gift certificates are in order. This gives another chance to change opinions through future work. For major repairs, perhaps it's best to trade into a different vehicle?   Structure the second deal correctly and everyone wins.

If mishandled, complaints feel like dragging a cinder block around the showroom floor – stabbing harmony's chest with a dull blade.   Furthermore, we disperse our frustrations across coworkers, customers, and loved ones at home.

How resourceful are you? Prove it, Champ.

Handle problems well. These situations separate you from others, so shine through resourcefulness and the ability to come up with solutions that work for everyone. Be quick to rectify dealer error, but gray area (much more common) means sitting down to figure things out rather than a flat, "No. Sorry we cannot help you."

These situations are the most difficult that the auto industry creates and very few individuals can handle them (managers or salespeople). The Blank Paper Method can easily raise your value to the dealership.

Do-Not-Do List – items are minor on the irritation scale, but escalate quickly if continued. Thus, punching harmony squarely in the nose.

1. Walking customers into desking or finance areas
2. Lot drops
3. Wearing non-uniform items
4. Smoking outside of designated areas
5. Cell phone use outside of approved areas
6. Last to speak to customer

Walking customers into busy areas is disrespectful to busy managers and depending on what's laying around, it may be against regulations. Sensitive items such as SSN numbers and credit reports should stay out of reach. Introduce prospects to managers by sitting them down and bring the manager over, rather than the other way around.

What is a lot drop? When a prospect drives through the lot and the salesperson fails to get them on the Road to the Sale, or obtain contact information. *Cue Plan B*: Get a name, number, and vehicle of interest. Managers expect pushback about always getting prospects inside, but we expect that your skills are good enough to get basic information. Leads are the fruits of advertising dollars and lot drops bruise the budget. Even if management aren't Lot Nazis and don't say anything about this behavior – *trust me* – fellow salespeople take notice.
<gritting teeth>
Squandering opportunity is a major irritation.

*"Why didn't they let someone else attempt the sale,
if they are going to be sloppy?"*

Granted, some customers make a pit bull look like a pet goldfish – but repeated failures send a very clear signal: Disrespect.

Also, many prospects drive through lots looking for specific vehicles. They are harder to get on the Road to the Sale, so salespeople get in the habit of bouncing these prospects without gathering information. Often, prospects drive through dealership lots looking for a specific vehicle and if they don't see it, they move on to the next lot. What happens if Mike wanders in looking for a Foreign SUV on Friday and a nice snazzy one arrives Monday morning? Rather than driving around town searching for Mike, search for a wooden door instead – insert head and close repeatedly (wood is more forgiving that metal), because both activities produce the same headache. Mike is in the wind.

Wearing non-uniform items makes a statement: I don't care about being on the team, even if your heart says otherwise, refusing to look like a teammate says otherwise.

Smoking outside of designated areas excludes customers you could otherwise enjoy selling. Some folks are sensitive about smoking and won't deal with a smoker. Likewise, ownership considers it disrespectful, so smoke in permitted areas.

Cell phones give off the wrong impression. Never, by any means, use your cell phone while speaking with customers. *Silly question, Champ.* If on a date, would you accept a call from tomorrows date? *Well, no.* This leaves a bad taste in your current prospects mouth. Hey, we can still use phones, after all, phones are an important sales tool – be resourceful and find a private place.

Being the last one to speak to a customer, especially when new, doesn't sit well with managers. Respect advertising investments by allowing a second set of eyes and ears to evaluate each person.

What goes around – comes around. Contrary to popular belief, the sales floor isn't a haven for backstabbers that relish the opportunity to take advantage of customers and coworkers alike.

Are some people like this?

Sure, every industry has bad apples and this is no different.   As a rule, these cats are short-lived because leadership is sensitive about things that bruise harmony, or coworkers' team up and reject people that don't play well with others.

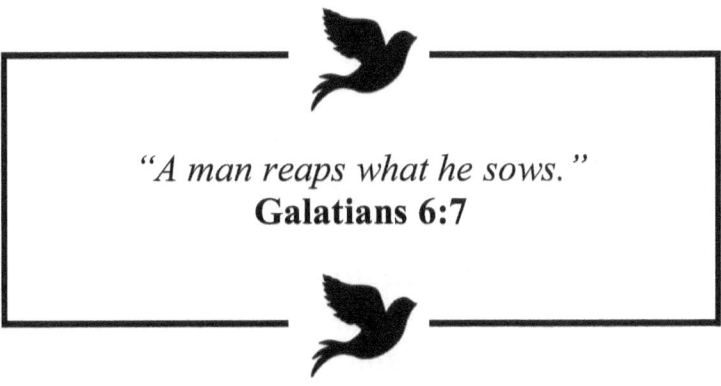

"A man reaps what he sows."
Galatians 6:7

This verse hits the Karma nail squarely. Man sows good: He reaps good. Man sows bad: He reaps bad. What goes around → comes around. Add good things to the team and the team opens their arms, brings you in, and embraces you.   Snatch every morsel within reach and turn your back on team dynamics and the ground rejects your seed.

Not, good.

Little things, like helping line up the lot, removing snow from cars, and helping with promotional items make a loud statement: I am part of the team. Bigger things like making sure a prospect gets in touch with a requested salesperson, taking good messages, or putting your best foot forward when working with someone else's customer comes back around when the shoe is on the other foot.

Furthermore, it's not just the team that reacts differently – the whole world does. A clean Spirit and positivity will attract others through good energy expelled. Yet, other things are difficult to label – those who have accepted God's Helper, the Holy Spirit, understand this concept yet cannot fully explain it. The bible says that His Spirit is available to anyone that requests it – once "downloaded" that Helper helps us navigate through the life's waters. Sometimes this Helper is like a rudder steering clear of danger and other times it steers us into opportunities.

"He will give you another
Helper to be with you forever."
John 14:16

In closing, it takes a keen eye to recognize harmony's effects. Something completely lost on many dealerships and businesses. Leadership mistakenly assumes that the strength of their team lies in individual ability – although strong individuals are good – they only produce their own output. Harmony enables the team to produce synergy. Through synergy, smaller stores outperform bigger ones. Through synergy, we can do more with less. And through synergy, we create that elusive "buzz".

Synergy — *an outcome that is greater
than all the parts combined.*

Hey, wouldncha mind speakin' English? Ok, fair enough. Let's take a crack at explaining this complex dynamic through something simple, like pulling horses.

Saddle up, partner.

Noel, hooks to the sled and pulls 500 pounds. Carol, hooks up to the same sled and pulls 500 pounds as well. What if we hook them together? How much would they pull? Easy math, and a smidge of commonsense, says if we hook them together, they should max out at 1,000 pounds – instead they hunker down and pull 1,500 pounds.

Hmmm... Interesting.

How is the extra output explained? *Synergy.* An outcome that is greater than all the parts combined.

Back to the happiest place on earth: Dealer Land.

Let's convert synergy to our sales floor. Elmer clips along and merrily sells 12 units a month. In a crazy scheme to sell more vehicles (insert sarcasm), Dahlberg Motors hires another salesperson. Eileen joins and she averages 12 units per month as well. They get together, ~~work on making babies in the closet~~ the buddy system and T.O for each other

201

– wait for it – and work in harmony. Their production boosts to 15/mo. each. Next, Elmer and Eileen recognize how to help managers keep their plates clean and working on key tasks, they in turn, become more productive and it bumps their monthly average to 18/mo. Meanwhile, leadership's confidence grows and they add more prospects to the system, *and voila!* 25 units per month! Elmer and Eileen went from barely above average to industry leaders.

Onlookers mistakenly assume these high producer's results is from individual ability – and it is – but not 100% sales-skills-related ability. Sure, some of their sales are credited to skills, but it's so much more. They understand harmony and connect the dots on helping the system run better, which cycles back around to help produce extraordinary results.

Chapter *Eight*

Organized

Kaysa and Nick sell cars at North Motors. Kaysa takes organization seriously. Her desk is clutter free and files neat – *hey*, she isn't perfect but makes an effort to keep organized. Nick, on the other hand, doesn't see the value in such things and lives in the moment. He piles things on his desk and refuses to throw things away. "I might need this one day, and I'm more concerned about selling cars than upkeep. I'm retail not detail – leave me alone." Nick justifies shortcutting because he is "too busy". As a result, things slip through Nick's hands and he misses opportunities. He sells 15 vehicles a month but has to work with 60 prospects. Kaysa, on the other hand, only needs 35 prospects to sell 15 vehicles.

Who is more valuable as an employee?
Well, duh. Kaysa.

This seems like a no-brainer but is completely lost on salespeople and managers alike. Leaderboards tally sold units only, thus displaying that nick and Kaysa are equal. Salespeople, especially new ones, measure progress on sales only, thus ignore a massive piece of the puzzle. Through organization, Kaysa produces with less leads.

Here lies the problem: *High failure rate.*

The average salesperson fails seven out of every ten times, consequently creating a mountain of follow up. New salespeople waltz to the sales floor and bounce off of 30-60 prospects – easily managing their follow up. The second month rolls around and they handle another 30-60 prospects and start to feel the weight of follow up. By the end of the third month, 90-180 prospects and are swimming through Hanging Deal Land. Over time, disorganization threatens to sink the ship.

Being effective revolves around being organized – and having a plan.

"Prepare your work outside; get everything ready for yourself in the field and after that build your house."
Proverbs 24:27

Prepare the little things before tackling larger things.

In sales, our main tasks are selling products and managing the customer base, everything else is secondary. We prepare our field by getting organized, and staying organized.

Accomplish this with the three P's: Planning, process, and priceless data.

Planning – our next day starts the night before so make a quick to-do list while it's still fresh in your mind before going home. In addition, maximize your day by using a four-chunk activity schedule to structure workdays.

Morning open - 8:30 a.m.
    Morning Prayer
    Work service drive
    Hawk potential trades (2-3 days per week)

Mid-Morning 8:30 -10:00 a.m.
    Morning meeting
    Get vehicles ready for appointments
    Complete calls and emails
    Training and role play (2 weakest skills)

Busy Hours 10-5 p.m.
    Hawk lot
    Work appointments
    Contact Prospects
    Reject non-sale-producing activity

Before Leaving
    Next day to-do list
    Update CRM
    Pray before going home
    (have teenagers? Pray twice.)

The 4-chunk schedule maximizes production *and* increases the quality of time at work. We generate income through selling products so a major portion of the day focuses on selling.

Waiting for prospects feels awkward: *Am I being lazy because I'm not doing anything but waiting?* This self-doubt is unsettling because we want to be productive and pull our weight – especially within view of the boss.

Lean forward and listen up Champ: *Lot coverage is your job.*

Don't fret about such things. Make follow up calls (within view of the lot), or walk around the lot rather than sitting still (for you, not the boss). Management doesn't frown upon being attentive to the lot – they do frown when prospects leave without interaction from salespeople.

The Four-Chunk Schedule prevents being drug down by non-result-producing material during busy hours. Many things surface throughout a workday and allowing them to swallow your time eats into your production level – high producers are masters at setting things aside and handling them during slow times. Handle anything non-sales related before 10 a.m. or after 7 p.m. During busy hours, be 100% focused on selling cars or preserving the customer base.

Process – use processes already built rather than building new ones. No need to reinvent the wheel – simply roll it. The workday revolves around three main processes.

- ✓ Road to the Sale (Chapter Three)
- ✓ Unsold Follow Up (Basic Skills Chapter)
- ✓ Sold Follow Up (Basic Skills Chapter)

Stay organized and productive by sticking to these key processes and doing them during the correct times to maximize time spent at work. Outperforming others comes from operating process, building rapport, sales skills, and a heavy dose of your personal flavor along the way, *not* from reinventing the wheel. Reject the mindset that it takes a high-tech, super-duper system to outperform others.

Priceless data - Customer data is the dealerships most valuable asset worth more than the inventory, building, or equipment inside. As mentioned, each customer represents a new branch and infinite possibilities of future sales – failure to get accurate data is like sawing off that branch and watching it fall to the ground. If working with CRM, input a test client and write down the required fields and collect those fields with every customer so there's no temptation to add gibberish when adding actual clients. *Oh, OK.* It's easy to get lost in the moment and ~~fabricate~~ forget to gather all the required information. As a result, the high dollar CRM gets loaded with made up data – rendering it less effective. *Boo!*

Priceless data's value is twofold: Follow up and future prospecting. Chase down customers with multiple forms of contact information such as work number, cell number, and email. Each sold represents a mountain of energy – think of how many prospects it takes to generate just one sale – so clutch accurate data like a beginning swimmer to the edge of the pool.

In addition, it takes advertising dollars to land each prospect within arm's reach. Maximize resources by collecting valid data and then use that data to keep producing fruit. Once capturing accurate data, our marketing costs are reduced.

FLASHBACK:

The market crash of 2008 reduced traffic to a trickle, we buckled down and got creative – do more with less became the mantra. Reduce advertising. Reduce inventory. *Reduce peaceful sleep.* The combination of fewer prospects and reduced inventory made for ~~panic~~ interesting times. Our dealership increased production partly due to priceless data. If we didn't have a prospects exact vehicle desired then we tried selling a vehicle closest to their goals. If that didn't work, we slid to plan C: Contact existing customers and try upgrading them into newer vehicles.

"We have a possible buyer for your vehicle. We won't buy outright, how do you feel about trading? This effectively turned one deal into two. Impossible to do without keep accurate data.

Why does it have to be slow to use this tactic?

Meanwhile, providing vehicle history makes the sale easier, so be resourceful and dip back into your own customer base whenever possible. Consider this:

> Kiah sold many vehicles to the Herrman family, new vehicles for Mom and Dad and budget vehicles for the new drivers. Kiah works with Loni, a fresh prospect, and Loni insists on buying a Chrysler Sebring convertible – a quick walk through the inventory turns nothing up. Kiah remembers selling one to the Herrman family a few years back and convinces them to bring it down. The Herrman's decide to upgrade because they received more for their Sebring than normal, and Loni gets the car she wants – Kiah makes two sales instead of one, and Loni is willing to pay a little more because Kiah can tell her the vehicles history.

Hasn't Kiah created a condition that only she could fulfill? Salespeople that provide background add value to the sales pitch. Through data collection and keeping it organized, a resourceful salesperson is able to do more with less. *Cue harps.*

Prediction: Grasp the three P's and produce more sales with less traffic and your value will increase ten-fold. Granted, dealerships are result driven beasts – often patting a person on the back for outselling the next place by one unit, but eventually leadership takes notice. Good things follow. Training others, coordinating events, and a higher level of trust just to name a few. Furthermore, take great pride in being organized – it's not easy – and like any other important thing, it's not supposed to be.

Chapter *Nine*

Metrics

*"Unequal weights are the abomination of the Lord,
false scales are not good."*
Proverbs 20:23

This verse hits the honesty nail square on its head. Many industries trust scales or measurements to evaluate conditions. Sometimes scales determine whether a harvest is successful, and other times their used to set portions. Many industries use scales to measure effectiveness.

Our scales are stats.

Without stats, we cannot track progress and quickly identify weak areas. High failure rate and prospect individuality combine to create mass confusion. Salespeople are at high risk for stalling growth because it's too hard to evaluate performance on the average workday alone. Prospects rarely give us a complete picture and we resort to grabbing our white canes and probing around until we form a clear customer picture. When the prospect leaves, unsold, the second-guessing begins and leaves us wondering whether we probed the right areas or missed something entirely. Stats bring the picture in focus and *True Scales* help navigate – no longer bound by:

"They were just looking."
"We didn't have what they were looking for."
"Mars, Jupiter, and Uranus are not at a perfect 18-degree angle."

These, and other, justifications slump to the canvass like a boxer that just forgot a third of his childhood through metrics. Stats reveal performance by comparing our average to industry average and store average.

"They were just looking."
"The stats show that you worked with 20 prospects and only sold 2 vehicles. The average salesperson sells 6 after speaking with 20."
"Yeah, but, they we're all just looking."
"Your coworkers are hearing the same thing and getting them inside and get them on to the Road to the Sale and use it to sell 3 out of every ten prospects they talk to."

Even though self-doubt never ceases (veterans suffer too), through stats, we step back and recognize struggles and address them rather than sticking our head in the sand. Regardless if your dealership is stat Nazi, *you* should be diligent in collecting stats because ultimately, it's you who has the most at stake.

A salesperson's stats are much like a racer. Setup the car (training) → runs laps (working leads) → record lap times (closing percentage) → adjust car (targeted training) → improved lap times (better closing percentage). Use closing percentage to measure performance. Beginning racers, don't measure success by whether they are leading the race – they measure lap times, but as a driver matures, we measure success by how they compare to the rest of the field. Like racers, new salespeople aim to improve closing percentage but eventually grow to topping leaderboards.

Keep stats for each lead source. This identifies strengths and weaknesses specific to the lead source, which helps targeted training. Gina's closing percentage is a sluggish 20% after her first month, evaluating stats she identified phone ups as a weak spot, and learns to handle them better. The adjustment increases her closing percentage to 28% – even though she is still under industry average, we're satisfied about the growth.

Every Monday, grab lasts week's registrations, separate them by lead source, and update your Monthly Stat Sheet.

Slow feet are sick feet.

Reviewing data weekly speeds up behavior changes and accelerates the learning curve. Gina's diligence, and quick feet, helps correct issues before they get out of hand. In addition, stats extinguish her self-doubt, leaving her focused and heading the right direction.

Tucker sees a stack of unsold prospects and convinces himself not to be concerned. I tried, and couldn't sell them. Gina sees a stack of 20 unsold prospects and calculates her closing percentage (sales divided by leads). Her four sales equal a closing percentage of 20%, knowing the average is 30%, she eyes that stack of unsold prospects differently: *I know there are at least two deals sitting in my follow up, I need to flush them out.*

212

Keeping Stats – for those not using a CRM, keep stats by saving your needs assessments forms. The 'How did you hear about us section' provides the lead source. Every week sift through the leads and tally them up on the Monthly stat sheet.

Even though we tally leads weekly, dealership staff lives month to month. Every new month cleans our slate and starts fresh numbers. Keep a snapshot of the previous month to have data to for growth review.

Monthly Stat Sheet

Source	Leads	Sold	Closing %	Goal
Walk In				30%
Repeat				80%
Referral				50%
Phone Ups				30%
E-Leads				10%
Prospecting				
Service Ups				
Total				
Monthly Income				
YTD Income				
Ave Per Sold				

Skills

(Circle two weakest skills every month)			
Objection Handling		Unsold Follow Up	
Phone		Sold Owner Follow Up	
Closing		Product Knowledge	
Walk Around		E-Leads	
Worksheets		Road to the Sale	
Referrals		Service Leads	

The Monthly Stat Sheet (top) provides data, and the Skills Sheet (bottom) provides solutions. The goal column displays industry standard closing percentages – use those, or your dealership's percentages to determine performance.

Monthly Performance Review – Sit down with your Sales Manager at the end of every month and review stats. Normally, staff avoids performance reviews as wood avoids the sander, but this activity creates healthy communication at the highest level. Stop and consider the message this sends:

"Can you give me a minute and look over my numbers and help point me in the right direction?"

The Sales Manager opens her sunglass case, removes her sunglasses, and slides them on from the blinding halo radiating above your head.

In addition, reviews give the opportunity to connect and work towards common goals. It's hard to see the forest from the trees and a second set of eyes helps identify issues. Regardless how good a salesperson is, he or she always has a weakest skill. If your dealership doesn't have this level of support, no sweat, get with a coworker and act as eyes and ears for one another.

Here are red flags and their solutions.

Red Flag	Solution
Closing percentage Too Low	More rapport building Better needs assessments Build better value – transfer excitement Worksheet training Work on closing techniques
Closing Percentage Too High	Refusing to work with difficult customers Train on Walk Away – get prospects inside Enter ALL leads
Low Repeat Sales	Train on Sold-Owner Process Target spouses Identify entire household needs Better rapport building

214

Low referrals	Train referral system Better rapport building Increase prospecting
Average gross Too Low (<1000)	Train on Walk-Around Attempt higher 1st and 2nd pencils Better rapport building
Average Gross Too High (>2000)	Accept lower profit deals Discount 3rd pencils more
Low Phone Ups (or closing %)	Train phone skills Giving price without assessing needs Not adding data into system
Low E-Leads	Need E-Lead training Giving price without qualifying Poor computer skills Poor phone skills

Goals Setting – is a source of frustration. The problem is twofold: Either there's no goal setting or no planned action to reach the goal. Salespeople that don't set goals are like arrows released without aiming. Whereas, salespeople that set goals without plotting action is like pointing at the target without firing. Both are more effective when setting realistic goals and understand what it takes to achieve them.

Unit Goals:
"My goal is to sell 20 cars this month."
"My goal is to top the leader board."
These are great goals but *how?* What's the plan to get there?

One way is to use your closing percentage and average days per month to calculate the number of leads needed per day to hit the goal.

Example:
    Goal = 20 sales
        67 (leads) x .30 (closing percentage) = 20 sales.
        67 (leads) /22 (working days) = 3 leads per day.

    Goal = 30 sales
        100 (leads) x .30 (closing percentage) = 30 sales.
        100 (leads) /22 (working days) = 4.5 leads per day.

By reducing goals to a simpler form, we increase the chance of obtaining it. Set a target and back into your daily needs – just as I did with the example. *Long sigh.* Yet, this isn't my preferred method.

Anyone smell a potential problem brewing?

This method begs the question: What about other salespeople? Surely. *they* have goals too. No biggie, just beat them to every prospect, right?
Yikes!
Why are all my coworkers sharpening their pencils and hawking my ears? *Hmmm.* And what about the customers? Beating coworkers to prospects feels great until you realize the wide-eyed prospect feels like a piece of meat – *sheesh* – talk about bad first impressions. That hurdle should be super fun to jump.

Cue downward departure on closing percentage.

Setting daily goals is fine, but traffic is outside our control. Cut the umbilical cord by creating your own leads through repeat, referral, and prospecting. Waiting on lot traffic is reactive and creating your own leads is proactive – combining both is the path to achieving goals.

Set activity goals for better results.

Here are some ideas:

- ❖ Goal of: Sitting by the phone while watching the lot to grab phone ups.
- ❖ Goal of: Asking every sold for referrals.
- ❖ Goal of: Working the Service Drive three days per week.
- ❖ Goal of: Using the 4-Chunk System and hawk the lot during busy hours.
- ❖ Goal of: Attending one prospecting venue per week (expert within the circle).
- ❖ Goal of: Setting up one event per month (indirect prospecting).
- ❖ Goal of: Cold Calling 20 leads per day (direct prospecting).

Notice that we transitioned to things within our control. Traffic is outside our control and highly irregular so setting goals in those areas can be frustrating.

Let's try our hand at income goals.

Income Goals: "I want to make $100,000 per year." Sounds great, Cletus, but *how?*

Take your average commission and divide the income goal, which equals the number of units needed.

Example:
Yearly Income Goal = $100,000
Average Commission (each person varies) = $488
$100,000 divided by $488 = 204 units
204 divided by 12 months = 17 per month
17 divided by .30 (closing rate) = 57 prospects
57 prospects divided by 22 = 2.5 prospects per day
(The average month has 22 working days)

The highlighted factors vary with each person and drastically skew results. For example, reducing the average commission amount to $300 means we have to sell 28 units per month rather than 17 – this is a major increase and not likely. Raise the closing percentage and we reduce the needed prospects. For example, raising it to 50% (a veteran's percentage) means we only have to work with half the leads. These factors affect results so drastically that it's more productive to focus on them rather than hovering around a calculator.

Before we trot too far on our income horse,
come back down here for a second.

Income driven goals are shallow – hang with me here – there is greater value in personal-growth goals than income goals. *I get it*, income is important; mortgage lenders don't take payment in the form of, "My communication skills with low-credit-score prospects has improved dramatically." However, focusing on income reduces the amount of energy that could've been spent in a more productive place: *personal growth*. Additional money is a byproduct of personal growth, therefore investing energy into personal growth is time well spent. *And yes*, personal growth almost always equals higher income.

Aim at factors that create the biggest impact. For example, increasing rapport skills ripples throughout the system in a positive way: Higher gross, more referrals (higher closing percentage and higher gross), and more repeat sales. Common ground, better control tactics, and teaming up skills influence the quality of rapport, which leads to higher compensation.

218

- ❖ Repeat and referrals skills – increases gross and closing percentage.

- ❖ Walk around Skills – builds excitement and value which raises closing percentage and gross.

- ❖ Worksheet Skills – raises closing percentage and gross.

- ❖ Closing Skills – increases volume.

- ❖ Phone skills – reduces walk-in dependency and increases volume.

Again, notice that we focus on things within our control. Straight Income goals have uncontrollable factors. For example, commission is based off dealership profit – so what if the inventory is tanked or the appraiser puts peanuts into every trade? Dwelling on these factors isn't healthy. In fact, doing so dilutes your priceless attitude and risks ruining more than paychecks.

Hey wait a minute, where did my wife and kids go?
Your attitude stinks mister, they left.

Therefore, place energy where it benefits you the most – on the things you can control: Skills, attitudes, and knowledge.

To some, tending the Sales Floor is a chore – yet others eye that real estate completely different: A place to display skills and prove how different they are from others.

I recommend setting goals that fuel a deeper significance than money. A Spirit-filled salesperson looks forward to serving our brothers and sisters and are rewarded accordingly.

In closing, *True Scales* please the Lord so be disciplined enough to keep stats and then use those scales to measure performance. Stat-based adjustments foster growth and keep a person on the right path rather than second guessing – prune unhealthy activity before it infects the trunk.

Chapter *Ten*

Types of Buyers

NEWSFLASH: The Auto Sales industry is brutal to learn. *Well, duh.* Oh, MY BAD – you already knew that? Ok, *well why?* Why is the employee failure rate so high? Even those that push past the first 90 days still limp home with clumps of missing hair. *Why?* Tyrannical bosses, pathetic training programs, and rude prospects surely don't help (*sheesh,* where do I get an application?) – But that's not all.

The different types of buyers shove many salespeople over the edge.

Monday morning, we have a successful sale and the person leaves completely satisfied. *Pluck the harp strings and open the wine bottles!* Later that afternoon we handle the next buyer the same way and are met with a shriveled nose, and clenched fists. Checking the bottom of your shoes isn't needed but examining the type of buyer you're dealing with is.

We'll show how to identify each type of buyer, our goal, and solutions to help close them.

- ❖ Heavy Shopper
- ❖ Boastful Buyer
- ❖ Tough Customer
- ❖ New Car Buyer
- ❖ GMD Buyer
- ❖ Logical Buyer
- ❖ Emotional Buyer

Heavy Shopper

How to Identify – The Heavy Shopper won't purchase until they've combed through data from multiple sources, hit the road to check things out, got an expert or two involved, and verified the location of the North Star (*yeah, seriously*). Identify these cats by their bulging research folders, which are stuffed full enough to shame a hoarder's trunk.

Pass the handkerchief – it's gunna get dusty.

Goal – Become part of their process, meaning slip into their system rather than starting a new one. After completing the needs assessment step, draw out their data and digest it. *Gulp.* Often, there's enough information to choke a whale and they desperately need help deciphering.

Sammy Salesperson, please step forward.

Become the leader. Build rapport and show the Heavy Shopper that you can be their trusted source.

Solution – Online reviews, manufacture propaganda, and dealer advertising all muddy the water – add thousands of choices – and screech! Doubt bares its teeth and sinks them into quick decision-making.

The Heavy Shopper struggles to tread water in a flooded pool of choices. Take control and exclude vehicles (based off your needs assessment) one by one until your left with two vehicles. Show the remaining two vehicles and turn it into an emotional or preference decision.

Heavy Shoppers are web savvy and heavily scrutinize price. Prices higher than an internet posting must be justified, such as fewer miles or more options. Being close to these advertised prices is usually enough to get the deal.

Boastful Buyers

How to identify – Boastful buyers love bragging about all the notches he or she (usually he) has on their negotiating stick (hung near the head-butting trophies).

WARNING: These fellas will drive you nuts!

Hang in there, Champ. There is a nice reward for the initial headaches.

Think Rodney Dangerfield. Except he's not heckling little leaguers, you're the target – loud, proud, and obnoxious. Furthermore, there's always a friend that doubles as audience, surely there to attest to the brow beating. Your first clue that Loud Lloyd might be a Boastful Buyer the fact that he drug in his buddy Bill, which has no interest in buying a vehicle or giving input on the current purchase. Or, the exact opposite – Meek Mike, the buyer, barely says a word and Loud Lloyd is Mike's designated ~~driver~~ mouthpiece.

SIDE NOTE: The last store wasn't willing to put up with his shenanigans, hence barking near your desk now. Tuck that in your ~~chamber~~ back pocket.

Goal – Boastful Buyers are not happy until they've ran over a salesperson. Therefore, let him run you over and limit activity to the current step. *Hmmm.*

Registration step = get ran over but assess needs.

Walk around = get ran over, but build value and relate features to needs.

Worksheet = get ran over, but get an offer.

Inform your manager early that you are dealing with a ~~ass~~ rambunctious person and they may need to get involved, so there are no surprises later.

Solution – These cats relish the negotiation so leave enough room to discount a few times and still hold profit in the end. Thankfully, these fellas don't research much (can't offer half price on web service?), so it's unlikely that your competing with some dealers hail damaged price 1200 miles away.

Start High → Discount Multiple Times → Don't Extended the Offer → Keep Worksheet

Extending the offer, means allowing the same price in the future – common for most customers, but allowing Mr. Dangerfield to leave with the worksheet enables him to browbeat the next person in his path and the competition sells him for a nickel less. *Um, hell no.* Make the price good for now only, and don't make a copy of the worksheet. If that doesn't work, create urgency by giving an additional discount if they buy within an hour.

Have a little fun with the exceptionally harsh ones. *Huh,* whatcha talkin' bout? Dig in, be resourceful, roll up thou sleeves, and ~~fight fire with fire~~ engage playful mode. Push these dogs back on their heels through creativity and make a game out of it. For example, set their vehicle near the frontage with "liquidation vehicle" written on the windshield while you're inside negotiating. If they play hardball and leave, dress the vehicle in 40 balloons, slap its rear, and park it out front. They want a story to tell... so give 'em one.

224

Hey, wait a minute.
Didn't you mention something about a reward for winning these cats over?

Pull up a chair this is where it gets good. Once these abrasive fellas have someone willing to dicker, they spread the word and 'help' others buy as well, which has zero to do with getting a friend or family a good deal, but everything to do with showing out.

Regardless, we *lurve* dem deals – bring 'em in!

"Bad bad" says the buyer,
but when he goes away, he boasts.
Proverbs 20:14

Our Father rebukes these same buyers. *Veeery interesting.*

The Boastful Buyer softens on future deals, especially if there are only a few dealers to choose from in the area – many won't tolerate Boastful Buyers. Thus, bringing a steady flow of prospects, and becoming an unpaid salesperson working on your behalf.

\<superhero cape flapping\>

Tough Customer

How to Identify – Our industry is stuffed with people that couldn't earn trust while holding a water hose next to a burning building.

Cue world's smallest violin.

Therefore, buyers play it safe by withholding trust from *any* salesperson – *including the good ones.*

Tough customers are ~~bullies~~ walking brick walls, which tests even the sharpest skills. The first red flag is rejected rapport-building attempts. Tough Customers take small talk, assessing needs, and humor and promptly place under their shoe and squash them like vermin. Furthermore, they go to great lengths to withhold information. Getting payment or money down goals is like pulling teeth. Throwing a trade in at the end of a deal is a common tactic as well.

"Do you have a trade in?"

"No."

Two hours later, and after going back and forth three times negotiating price, *then* comes a trade.

"I'd do the deal, but I need to get $1,000 over retail for my Huffy bicycle."

Goal – Warm up cold buyers through good energy. If rude, put your foot down, which is a hair raising and very much an ALL-IN bet, it goes like this:

"Hey Bud, have I done something to offend you?"

Which returns a blank stare, or if a female is with, they will nudge Mr. Gruff. Then follow with, "Listen, I understand not liking salespeople, my family hates salespeople and I spent most my life avoiding them as well.

226

Honest salespeople run circles around the slicksters and I take great pride in being different, so loosen up and give me a chance, and I promise to take good care of you."

Interesting enough, I've never had it backfire and lose a deal. <knocking on wood>

Push back and their wall tumbles. Folks respect this behavior, which allows you to get your foot in the door and build rapport. Not to be confused with in their space and glaring nose to nose – instead, be resourceful and push back in a healthy way.

Solution – Strap up, Champ. We're going to knock us down a Tough Customer. No, no, not the muzzleloader – that's too much firepower – your little old slingshot will do just fine David.

Draw out the things the Tough Customer is sensitive to and then side step them. This question reveals a wealth of information, "Why didn't you buy at the last dealership you visited?"

➢ They wanted to pull my credit before looking at a vehicle.

➢ They wanted to go back and forth, I don't do that.

➢ They would only give me $2,500 for my trade, it's worth $2,650.

➢ The manager requested that I take off my class ring before pummeling the salesperson – *I refused.*

Wait for it – Avoid making the same mistakes as the last dealer, which is much easier alter they're pointed out, agreed? So mark the landmines!

Reload the slingshot, we're not done yet.

Next, fire up the character machine and prove you're not like other salespeople – this won't happen quickly.

HINT: *Actions speak louder than words.*

Consequently, we (sales industry) engineered the Road to the Sale for exactly this type of buyer and it works very well for removing hesitation walls brick by brick. Throughout the process, we gain trust

- ❖ Registration = additional probing to completely understand needs.

- ❖ Walk-Around = thoroughly inspect the vehicle with the customer.

- ❖ Review inspection sheets and review work completed.

- ❖ Wash trade before appraisal.

- ❖ Worksheet = slow down and be thorough.

Kill with kindness and ~~lump hot coals on their head~~ have a softer customer during the worksheet step.

Ooooh, my.

Don't assume that a zero profit deal is the answer, because these buyers scoff regardless of the numbers so don't give away the farm just because you're looking at narrowed eyes, instead hold ye ground, Mate. Melting a

Tough Customer's frozen wall is very rewarding and gains loyal future customers.

Raving Fans, by Ken Blanchard, Sheldon Bowles, and Harvey Mackay gives great advice about certain customers. There's a sliver of population that will never be happy regardless of how far you bend over backwards. So, it's alright to refuse sales if the buyer is going to slander the dealer anyway. To the saleaholic (guilty) this is crazy talk – but after thousands of deals, the same darn pattern emerges.

Low profit deals = disgruntle customers.

I have zero issues with turning low-profit deals, but if the buyer stomps around and won't be satisfied regardless of effort (price and otherwise) then turning our back maybe in order.

Veeery few buyers end up in this category.

New Car Buyer

How to Identify – New Car Buyers like to upgrade every two or three years and always drive a vehicle under factory warranty. *Ah, yes.* The good life, mate. Pass the Piná Colada. Folks trading vehicles still under factory warranty are likely New Car Buyers.

Goal – New Car Buyers are fussy and get what they want. Start by getting a clear picture of options they would like and which options they are flexible on. And finally, land on vehicles closest to their goals. There is higher markup on used vehicles than new vehicles (*long sigh*). As a result, we're aggressive on trade values. In fact, New Car Buyers shop dealers against each other solely to get higher trade values – because new car dealers work from the same vehicle cost, trade values are often the deciding factor.

<batting eyes at appraiser>

Be thorough regarding trade details and give the appraiser ammo to stack additional money into the trade such as, proof of maintenance, the extra special luster shine added at delivery (rolls eyes), fabric protection, or extra accessories. Furthermore, make sure the appraiser knows that your customer is on a new vehicle and they will be aggressive.

Solution – New Car Buyers understand intricate rebates, special rates, or other manufacture incentives and prefer to cut to the chase when it comes to the numbers: "What is the to-boot amount?"

New Car Buyers wisely push aside these complex factors and want to know what the new vehicle costs in addition to giving their trade – To Boot.

For instance:
$20,000 Price
$2,500 Rebate(s)
$17,500
$12,500 Trade Value
$5,000 To Boot

Speak in to boot terms rather than stepping through each number of the equation. Comparing a competitors worksheet is ideal. Asking for it before going over numbers is ~~blissful~~ absolutely ideal – yet highly unlikely. New Car Buyers are usually savvy enough to withhold this information until after you've presented numbers. However, if you tickled rapport good enough to wet itself, then you may be able to pull this information out before showing numbers.

Cue huge advantage.

An appraiser that inspects the glove box area during their appraisal process would definitely, without a doubt... well, perhaps you'll figure that one out for yourself.

If your numbers are higher than the competition don't fret, simply ask what it would take to end his or her shopping, then take the offer back to your manager. Dealers love new car deals and work hard to get them – so hang in there.

Manufacture rebates vary depending on area, meaning the exact same vehicle has different rebates depending on what zip code the buyer lives in (*Booo!*), so it's absolutely crucial to determine accurate rebates. In addition, buyers may be entitled to specific rebates that only apply to him or her, so be thorough. This produces a lower to boot number without changing price or trade value.

Berry good, Danielson.

For instance, manufactures give extra rebates to Farm Bureau members or buyers who own a competitor's make, and If the competition uses more rebates, you could ~~look like an idiot~~ be at a considerable disadvantage. Thoroughness is your friend. Run rebate reports and review all the smaller individual rebates.

In closing, New Car Buyers are savvy buyers but they are also loyal buyers. This combination creates much confusion.

Case in point: Roxanne and Gary bought their last five F150's from their salesperson, Casey. Heck, they have a picture of Casey on their fridge and they see him every week at their kid's soccer games. When ready for a new truck, they don't blindly walk in, hand their keys over, and tell Casey to print the paperwork. Instead, they visit a few stores and get numbers – and keep Casey honest.

Hmmm, understandable.

Silly question though: What are those interactions like down at the other dealerships? They don't walk in and announce they intend to keep their dealer honest. *No, sir.* Instead, they act just like an actual buyer – with one major exception. They refuse to commit. Failing to understand this dynamic will have you tugging your hair out.

What the heck is going on here?
Why won't these people agree to purchase!

Engage What If strategies.

"What if I could get them to add $2,000 to your appraisal? Wouldcha do the deal?"

"Um, ah, um. No not today."

"What if I could get them to drop the price $5,000 more? Wouldcha buy it?"

"Um, ah, um. Well, can I get that in writing?"

If the customer initials an offer and says, yes, I will buy if certain terms are met. This is a very good sign. Go to work figuring out the sale. Refusing to initial offers, especially ridiculous ones is a red flag that they never intended to purchase.

Don't let these savvy buyers spin you out
and cause you to mishandle the actual buyers.

Overcoming Casey's ten-year's worth of sales is nearly impossible. Instead, create your own repeat buyers and attempt to be the salesperson that your buyers are bringing those glove box worksheets to.

GMD Buyer
Stands for "Get Me Done!"

Ways to Identify – This is the mantra for low credit score buyers. "I'll take whatever vehicle you can get me approved on." Obviously, we identify GMD buyers through checking credit, but not all GMD buyers know they have low credit scores. To make matters worse, credit score systems don't provide the same score as the dealers pull, like Credit Karma and similar services. Scores differ depending on which package the vender purchases, so if a customer checks his or her score at home, they have a number in mind when they get to the store – lenders score differently.

Sound confusing? *Yup*, hella confusing.

Why pout about credit vendors renovating their west wing with their additional fees (surely the reason for confusion)? *Maaaaybe*, we should just deal with it.

Most GMD Buyers are ideal buyers: Pleasant, thankful, and realistic.

Let's discuss the ones that are not.

Goal – Educate muscled up GMD Buyers inoffensively. Print a copy of their credit report, review it with them, and circle things that reduced their score. *Pass a slice of Humble Pie please.* Use facts, rather than emotions, to bring disgruntle GMD Buyers back to earth. Next, make sure they will accept the subprime lender's terms. At first glance, these terms are confusing.

- ✓ Five model years or newer
- ✓ Under 80k miles – preferably under 50k
- ✓ $325/mo. with at least $1,000 down

So lemmie get this straight – We're going to force GMD Buyers to take high payments, put cash down, and drive nice vehicles? *Well, yeah.* Some dealers lend their own money – dubbed Buy Here Pay Here. Those dealers require double or triple down payment, higher monthly payments, and vehicles with double the miles. *Ouch!*

Life's full of choices: (A) poor terms or (B) pay cash.

Some GMD Buyers are very conscious not to overextend themselves, and rightfully so, low payments mean "playing it safe". There is a much bigger dynamic in play. GMD buyers run a greater risk of repossession, which burdens the lender to resell the vehicle. Newer, low mileage vehicles are much easier to sell than older ones with high miles. *Oh,* ok. In addition, repairs are less likely on newer vehicles. And lenders know that when it comes to making payments or making repairs, it's the lender who gets ~~screwed~~ shortchanged. They prevent risk by forcing customers to buy nicer vehicles.

Feel free to disagree – but unless you are willing to provide loans at different terms – it is irrelevant.

Get GMD Buyers to view their circumstance as temporary and short-term. Our Creator, God, foresaw our weakness and came up with a system for forgiving debts and starting with a clean slate: *It is written* that every seven years our debts are cleared — as well as forgiving debts owed to us. Thousands of years later, this tradition lives on through bankruptcy (or dropping off our credit files).

Interesting, huh?

Move on from mistakes and reestablish.

Cue new loan.

234

Solutions – Closing GMD buyers is difficult because of the payment shock, and to make matters worse the money down required eliminates the security of just-in-case funds. Treat these buyers with the same level of respect as you would others – dealers are notorious for belittling GMD Buyers, and even if the customer is willing to take the terms, they refuse to do business with a dealer who treats them poorly. Communicate with a clean heart and don't cast stones.

1. Show a vehicle to build excitement (salt mouth)
2. Submit to lenders
3. Present options (provide water)

Some dealers refuse showing vehicles first. If the buyer falls in love with a vehicle the chances of them swallowing a high payment is much greater.

Logical or Emotional Buyers

The majority of buyers don't fall into the types we just discussed; they are the exception, not the rule. Most buyers tilt towards being emotional or logical decision makers, and by identifying each, we can communicate in a way that caters to their type.
Become a chameleon?
No, Champ. Never change who you are.

Allow your mojo to shine through warts and all – rapports foundation rests on authenticity, not perfection. Recognize which personality type you're dealing with, *and then draw more from your emotional side or logical side.*

For example, Shelly comes to the dealership and Russell, her salesperson, identifies her as an emotional decision maker. He shows her a Mountaineer and paints an emotional picture by discussing safe winter driving, the premium leather seats, and 3rd row seating to pile in all her ~~brats~~ grandchildren. Before signing out, Shelly brings back her husband Jay to check out the vehicle. Jay is a logical buyer. Russell changes his communication style. Instead, he talks about how the four-wheel drive system, low mileage, and fuel mileage improvement over her trade. By tailoring his presentations, Russell speaks both their languages and has an easier time moving to the worksheet step.

How to identify – Most buyers are Emotional Decision Makers – this isn't meant to be demeaning, heck, I'm one of them. *Pump the brakes, Champ.* We cannot assume that everyone is an Emotional Buyer.

Job type helps identify.

We ask for prospect's current employer early in the sales process (registration), so form an opinion early and then look for clues to see if they match the profile. Here are job types that are dominate in each:

Emotional	Logical
Salespeople	Teachers
Advertising	Engineers
Marketing	Military
Retail	Mechanics
Customer Service	Electricians
	Plumbers
	Construction

Beyond line of work, look at how a prospect describes the vehicle of interest. Do they paint a picture full of emotion driven needs, or stick to functional requests? Are they flexible and willing to explore many options, or sticking to pre-thought plan? How a person verbalizes their requests is a good indicator of buyer type.

Tips for Emotional Buyers – Emotional Buyers are much more receptive to a salesperson's pitch and therefore susceptible to the product behind the message (arched brow). They want to be "sold" and look forward to riding a purchase-driven high. Ditch dull deliveries and give this person what they want! Get excited and transfer that energy to the buyer. Deliver messages that pull at his or her feelings.

I loved when my salespeople bought new vehicles, *and no*, it had nothing to do with profit ($100 over cost). *Cue teachable lesson.* Let's see if we can transform full-grown adults into sparkle-eyed children with a new toy.

We moved around the vehicle with big smiles and high-fives. First, we climb inside and test the moon roof. Next, we fire up the upgraded sound system and nuzzle into the leather seats. Back outside, we check out the premium rims, release the tailgate, and touch every corner – by the time we finished, one would think I was the buyer, not them.
Aren't most salespeople Emotional Buyers?
Hmmm.
Would they connect the dots on how good a new purchase feels? *Hmmm.*

Ah, yes. The abuser becomes the abused.

Tips for Logical Buyers – These cats may not be as fun to sell to but at least they give us a clear path (long sigh). These detail driven buyers look to meet specific criteria, so take extra time to gather all of their requirements. Treat this list as your roadmap. *Select vehicles that fulfill those requirements.* Don't have an exact match? No sweat. Grab your closest two, present them, breakdown the advantages, and let them pick. Logical Buyers crave analyzing. Therefore, provide two pieces of meat to chew over – this moves the buyer from deciding to buy – to which one.

Well, ya dirty dog...

These buyers cough, sneeze, and develop hives whenever a sales pitch threatens to invade a conversation, so ditch them. Painting pictures irritates the Logical Buyer, instead skip to the end of your message and then come back and fill in the details.

Tell time: Then explain the clock.

In closing, high producers are masters at recognizing when to shift gears and pull from their emotional or logical side to connect with prospects at a deeper level. Remember, it's the little things that combine to make a big difference. People have choices coming out their wazoo and can do business with many dealerships.

"With all things being equal, people will do business with, and refer business to, those people they know, like, and trust."
-Bob Burg

Chapter *Eleven*

Industry Basics

Understanding dealership basics is crucial. This topic spins out many new recruits. *Cue elephant in the room.* Sharp-tongued managers please step forward. Rather than sugarcoating messages instruction comes is harsh and rude. ~~Arrogant~~ Overworked managers resort to short punchy answers, and I won't lie, a few managers almost drank their lunch through a straw during my days on the sales floor.

Guilty, Your Honor.

Yes, I did threaten to break that man's jaw.

Those jerks aimed at my precious egg!

Over time, I made an important connection: Managers don't make money unless my egg hatches, so my egg is also *their* egg. They are blunt about protecting their egg. *Oh, ok.*

Everyone's paycheck rests in their hands and properly staffed dealerships refuses to carry extra managers. Thus, spreading managers thin. *Does it justify being rude?* Not exactly, but after the dust settles so do managers and with a little work the auto industry becomes a very rewarding business.

Lean forward and listen up Champ
– this is where it gets good.

Something interesting happens after a salesperson stabilizes: They are worth more than a manager. *Not a typo.* A stable, high-producing salesperson is harder to replace, therefore worth more. A high-producer, meaning one who understands dynamics, prospects well, closes a high percentage of deals without help, and sells at least 20 units a month. Meanwhile, an interesting thing happens when problems surface: They get what they want. For example, if a loyal customer has a borderline issue the high performer gets bills covered whereas managers heavily scrutinize other requests.

Sharper pencils: *Done.*

Need extra time off: *Done.*

Managers polishing their shoes during lunch? *Don...* Well, only on Mondays.

What a great dynamic. Things return full circle and reward a high performer for doing things right. Not much different from exceptional sports players, is it? Please refrain from reaching full-brat mode, one who refuses to wait in line anymore but when your opinion is the most valuable in the room – good things follow (unless standing in a toddler's room, then, not so much). There is a great reward for dealing with mouthy managers: The minor buzzing of mosquitoes to eat years of good fruit.

Salesperson Compensation – Two tanksful of gas almost cost me over a million dollars, and more importantly, a deeply satisfying career. Please allow me to explain.

240

A local dealership manager staggered into the restaurant I worked at on a slow Thursday night and observed me interacting with patrons.

"You'd be great in sales." He kept repeating. "Why don't you come down and apply?"

Um, hell no.

After spending two years in tech school for a Computer Information Specialist, I dreamt of snuggling with the technology field. He explained that they just got a new computer system and maybe I could train others how to use it. *Hmmm.*

<nibbling the bait>

Friday afternoon, I wandered to the store and interviewed – for sales, not a computer position.

Ugh! Sales? Cue gag reflex. I hated salespeople.

They offered a base wage that was about two tanksful of gas difference than my current job. Ok, I accept, but only until the computer job opens up. A month later, I was hooked and loved every minute.

Had I not swallowed the fear of the unknown it would've cost me dearly. I shudder to think what would have happened had I refused that job. Rather than hide these embarrassing fears, it's fruitful to bring them up and address them head on.

This same fear cripples countless people from getting involved in an amazing industry.

Let's talk about compensation.

Straight Commission – The most common pay plan is 100% commission based. If you sell a vehicle for $11,500 and the dealership owns it for $10,000 then the dealer calculates commission based on $1,500 dollars in profit. If your commission rate were 25% (a common percentage) then your commission would be $375. An average month is 8 to 12 sales, which equals $3,000-$4,500. This clicks in at 36k-54k per year.

Not earth shattering – but these are *average* numbers.

Above-average performers easily pocket double those wages.

Commission Plus Base Pay – In addition to commission, some dealerships offer base pay. For example, $250/wk. plus 25% commission.

Draw – means advancing money and deduct it from future earnings. For example, the dealership pays $500 per week whether the salesperson sells a vehicle or not, and then deducts those amounts with future commissions.

Unit Based Pay – Best price stores (non-negotiating stores) use a unit-based pay plan rather than commission based. Tiers are set up whereas the more units the salesperson sells the higher the pay.

Spiffs – are bonuses paid for selling certain vehicles (usually aged), these units are usually zero or negative profit so managers give a flat rate of $50 - $1,000 dollars. Manufactures also incentivize selling certain new vehicles by paying salespeople directly.

Spouses love spiff checks, so if your spouse refuses his or hers, *feel free to send it over...*

Ask 100 salespeople which pay plan is best you would get 100 different answers (150 if college ED-a-ma-KATE-ed). After experience with nearly every pay plan, I prefer simple pay plans the best: Straight commission.

242

Simple pay plans help keep attention focused where it should be, the customers. Complicated pay plans force salespeople to hover around a calculator instead of customer's needs. *Boo!*

In addition, straight commission reinforces a self-employment attitude. Removing base pay reinforces "I've earned my compensation.", and removes friction for leaving the store (school functions, waxing back hair, or hiding from warrants). High performers always have their selling shoes on, even when outside the store, so missing a couple hours here and there is a valid trade off. The biggest advantage for straight commission is higher commission rates – forgiving base pay opens the door for higher commission percentages, which equals a higher upside. *Cue harps.*

Eventually, I upgraded to a straight commission pay plan and was scared to death for giving up a secured weekly paycheck. Why put myself at risk for not having a paycheck? These fears turned out to be a waste of time and energy. Proverbs 29:25 reveals the same message.

"The fear of man lays a snare, but whoever trusts the Lord is safe."

Still shivering? Alright Mate.

Individuals paid an hourly wage or a salary, are unable to make more than their wage allows. The reward for extra effort is a *chance* for promotion, or *maybe* a pat on the back. Many employers pay just enough so a person will not quit, and in return employees do just enough not to be fired.

Charming.

In contrast, commissioned employees have no ceiling as to what they earn in a single day, week, or month.

In addition, everything evens out on a long enough timeline. Silly question: If your current job switched to paying bi-weekly or monthly, would you panic?"

Um, no. Adjust and move on. Pull back the lens from weekly to monthly income, and it destroys the argument for "What if I can't pay my bills?"

Yes, it's true, salespeople have bad weeks.

We get past them and move on. Take this to the bank my friend: *It's very rare for a motivated salesperson's drought last longer than a week or two.*

Let's break down some numbers for an average salesperson.

	Week 1	Week 2	Week 3	Week 4	Total
Elmer	$750	$1,250	$100	$1,600	**$3,750**
Pete	$0	$2,000	0	$5,200	**$7,200**
Noel	$500	$250	$750	$2,750	**$4,250**
Salary Employee		$1,750		$1,750	**$3,500**
Hourly Employee	$875	$875	$875	$875	**$3,500**

These numbers highlight two points: Things even out over a longer timeline and the bottom two are ~~trapped~~ stuck. The top three examples will see income skyrocket with self-development – *with*, or *without* manager approval.

Salary and hourly employees are under management's complete control, they set wages, schedules, and work conditions – someone else dictates a major portion of their life. On the other hand, the top three incomes are driven from their own choices, they choose who gets their time and they are free to choose how to handle those people.

Right there, Cupid flung an arrow at my heart.

I fell in love with a ~~hussy~~ girl named Sales.

In closing, these factors magnetize the sales industry – repelling some and drawing others. Something amazing happens after salespeople get their footing: The hungry are fed a constant dose of growth because it's a mentor-driven industry.

Daily success and failure provides a constant shift between immediate gratification and mistake correction, which combines to produce an environment that very few industries can match.

I challenge you: Be open-minded, be different, and come strengthen an industry that needs Spirit-Driven People.

Acknowledgments

Claiming the content of this book as my own would be wrong. Like many others, I've granted hungry ears to many sales horses and learned many of these techniques throughout showrooms across the Midwest. I've caught these techniques while digging in the sales trenches and clung to them like a soldier clings to training, then added my flavor along the way.

This personalization blurs the line of origin, but I'm certain where I've learned a few concepts, and owe these people a great debt.

Jim Bozich.
Jeff Himmler
Chris Black. (ABQ Method),
Rick "Cup Cake' Krenzlok. (walk-around methods)
Joe Hengton.
Adam Tollers.

All these fellas dished out sales technique like a spewing volcano and anyone with ears stood stronger after watching them work. I am certain that these horses carried me past the normal learning curve at double the normal rate.
Thank you.

Jeff Himmler is the Dale Carnegie of desking and I got a front row seat on watching something special. During nearly 50 dealership sales events, Jeff gave me world-class lessons on holding gross, stretching for volume, and creating amazing culture. In addition, his discipline, encouragement, and leadership skills excelled him past being a great boss squarely into mentor land. Jeff's blessed hands developed hundreds of top-producing salespeople; many are now sales managers, GM's, and Dealership Owners. Propelling just a handful of these horses would be impressive. Developing them from scratch, meaning zero experience, is mind blowing. Doing it a hundred times over, all while running a newbie-filled sales team (good producers promoted into dealerships) *is unheard of*. Spending a year on the road travelling with Jeff to different events created lifelong fruits, personal and business.

Thanks Jeff.

Moving from short-term to long-term attitudes didn't happen overnight, nor did it happen on accident. Jim Bozich is a master at many things but none greater than teaching how to snuggle with buyers and think beyond the day. Most people know Jim as the calculated ~~animal~~ owner of a 20-store auto group, who can skillfully work a roomful of lions with a grandmother's touch. He spilled a thousand years of wisdom into his army of hungry GM's but the best lessons came when no one was looking.

Watching him interact with customers changed me.

Only a select few witnessed him roll up his sleeves and submit to customers one by one – which occurred at perfect timing in my sales career. After mastering rapport, sales process, and closing – Jim gave me the final ingredient: S*ubmitting* to customers. Without this insight, it would've taken me years to understand that true customer intimacy happens through submission.

Thank you, Jim.

A special thanks to my family – who, bless their heart – could have marker colored walls and catch me with inked fingertips and still hug me to bunches. *Cue the Rod*. My Grandparents are great leaders in our family circles and are the very definition of, "lessons are caught, not taught." I've caught pockets of wisdom throughout the years and hope my Grandchildren respect me half as much as I do them.

These words would've never found their page if it wasn't for Ryan Wilson, whose well-timed rebukes pushed me to keep writing, and learning (slightly faster that a plump goldfish), and more importantly, kept my spirits afloat amid major crisis. Ryan, and his Spirit-filled family, wrapped their arms around us and took us in as one of their own. God called him home early, and he passed before seeing the fruit of his efforts – meaning this book. Regardless, anyone within arm's reach of this family is blessed, including ours.
Thank you.

In closing, God blessed me with enough ability to beat my chest for all to see, but His power is best shown in weakness – and that's exactly when fell in love with Our Father's strength.
During weakness.
You carried your fallen son through crisis and I am forever in debt.
Thank you, Father.

"God provides the wind, but man must raise the sails."
— Augustine of Hippo

Suggested Readings

1. *Bible* – the bible acts at guideposts to keep us centered and moving forward on a healthy path. Digesting the bible won't happen in one reading (or a dozen); instead. God does a great job at meeting followers wherever they are. Today, we have hundreds of different religions and every time we split ourselves, it weakens our influence against the serpent. The bible lists only two religions: Believers and nonbelievers. I am the former and hope the bibles truths leads to peace in your heart just as it has done to mine.

2. *One Minute Manager Meets the Monkey*, Ken Blanchard – A must read for people that stretch themselves too thin and desperately need help cleaning their plate, and keeping it clean. Ambitious people can easily bury themselves. Take your life back in under an hour with this short book.

3. *Good to Great,* Jim Collins produced a top-shelf business book that focuses on sticking to areas of specialty and the importance of momentum. His chapter on the flywheel and doom loop is one of the most memorable chapters I have ever read.

4. *Tipping Point*, Malcolm Gladwell. This is a great read for understanding word of mouth advertising and highlights how the law or the few affects the masses. The author leaves no stone unturned and a great read for any retail worker.

5. *Rich Dad Poor Dad Series* – Robert Kiyosaki keeps delivering good book after good book. His series has

grown considerable over the years and anything he puts a pen to is worth reading. The original, *Rich Dad Poor Dad* and *Cash Flow Quadrant* are my favorites. All his books share an underlying theme of putting the desire to learn above attending college.

6. ***Richest man in Babylon***, Samuel Clason – This book does an amazing job of reducing complex money concepts down to language so simple that a child could understand. A must read for saving, protecting, and compounding your money. This book packs a wealth of information in a short compact book and I wouldn't hesitate laying it in a adolescent's hands and trusting that the concepts won't be lost on them.

7. ***How to Win Friends and Influence People***, Dale Carnegie – wrote this book on understanding people decades ago and it's still the gold standard for interacting with strangers today. This was the first adult book I laid in my children's hands and I bought 50 copies and gave them out to all my sales staff, friends, and family. I regret not buying 200.

8. ***Raving Fans***, Kevin Blanchard – defines exceptional customer service and motivates any hungry sales rep to look beyond traditional customer service and set yourself apart from others. In a world tripping over each other to get in front of customers, Raving Fans teaches us to build it – and they will come. In addition, I love how this book gives permission to refuse some business.

9. ***Sales Dogs***, Robert Kiyosaki – This book does a great job helping managers identify the different

personality types salespeople carry and unique ways they chase down sales. Managers are notorious for my-way-or-the-highway attitudes, and this book is a slap in the face to all the rigid, close-minded, bosses out there. I gave my salespeople more space to maneuver after reading this book and recognized my employees for their strengths rather than dwelling on weakness.

10. ***The Four-Color Person***, Max Luscher – this book is great for salespeople that need to quickly identify prospects personality types, once identified it shows how to cater to that individual rather than frustrate them with sales tactics that they don't respond to. Even though auto salespeople have a bigger window to work in, this book helps to avoid annoying certain buyers.

11. ***The Seven Habits of Highly Effective People***, Stephan Covey – lays down the gauntlet and challenges readers to understand what makes the high performers tick. Habits are at the center of our lives and Covey challenges us to rethink them.

12. ***4-Hour Body***, Timothy Ferris. Confession: I am a Timothy Ferris addict. He hooked me with 4- Hour Chef, pulled me in deeper with 4-Hour Work Week, and reeled me into his boat with 4-Hour Body. Anything this guy touches is worth reading. Specifically, 4-Hour Body teaches everyone from the big belly beard grower to the 90-pound Monk how to eat and take care of themselves better. Tim is a master at explaining concepts and giving systematic instructions backed with his own testing and stats. He also unveils food industry shenanigans and sheds

light on flaws in research, testing, and marketing games played by vendors. If you need an idiot-proof game plan, trust Tim Ferris to deliver one.

13. ***Tools of the Titans*** — Tim Ferris collects his mountain of resources and compiles it into one book. Interviews with industry leaders shed light on what makes the high performers tick. One could spend the next 10 years tugging on the shirtsleeves of influential people and not get half the knowledge that this book provides.

14. ***Principles of Persuasion,*** Dr. Robert Cialdini – Do you crave having a mirror into your psyche? This book reveals human nature and deeply embedded things that live inside each one of us. This book is too much to chew all at once, instead read one chapter and allow it to digest. Afterward you will have a much deeper understanding of human nature. Its concepts are at the core of effective selling.

15. ***The Way of the Superior Man***, David Delia – created an absolute masterpiece with this book giving clueless fellas (ME) insight into the complex female spirit. Either God blessed him with a window into the better half's soul, or a very wise female held his hand while writing this book. Either way, it's by far the best book I have ever read regarding understanding women. I would never claim to master the female spirit but after standing on this book, I can proudly look her in the eye.

16. ***The Five Love Languages***, Gary Chapman hangs the bait of connecting to our lovers in deeper ways, but indirectly this book teaches us how to understand

252

everyone better. A wise lover figures out their partners love language. A wise parent figures out their children's love language. A wise friend figures out their friend's love language. And a wise manager figures out their employee's love language. When we understand others around us, we connect at a deeper level and Mr. Chapman shows us the path.

17. ***How to Swim the Sharks without Getting Eaten Alive***, Harvey Mackey – teaches us how to be your competition's worst nightmare. Specifically, his chapter on settling into second place and waiting for the number one to slip is a game changer. This easy-to-digest book is a must read for anyone chasing sales, or accounts, down.

Reference Items

Process Sheet

Use the processes below or get with management to match them to your store.

Major Processes:
1. **Road to the Sale** → Meet and Greet Registration → Touch Desk → Pick Vehicle → Pull Vehicle up → Walk Around → Test Drive → Trial Close → Worksheet → Finance → Delivery.

2. **Sold Owner Follow Up**
   Day 1= Thank you call, and ask for referrals.
   Day 7= Invite back to review options.
   Day 30= Vehicle Preforming well?
   Birthday and Vehicle Anniversary Cards.
   Check in Every 6 months.

3. **Unsold Follow Up**
   Review Stalled Deals Daily
   Day 1= Thank you for coming in.
   Day 2= How is shopping going?
   Call every day until sold or dead.

4. **CRM Inputs** Enter first note using 1-2-3-4-5 system,
   1. Vehicle of Interest.
   2. Price, payment, and money down goal.
   3. Trade (Yr., Mk, Miles).
   4. Minutes from store.
   5. Credit Score.
   Add new notes with every contact (or attempted contact).

Secondary Processes:

1. Appraisals (sales) → Complete Appraisal Form → Pull vehicle to appraisal area → Give keys to appraiser → Fill out Sales Worksheet.

2. Appraisals (managers) → Pull AutoCheck → Pull Book Values → Inspect and Drive Vehicle → Value Vehicle → Add Values to CRM.

3. Fresh Trades → Make New Key Tag → Use Stock number from sale vehicle adding next letter to end → Park in Raw Materials → Give Keys to Service.

4. Pulling Credit – signed registration form → Login to Dealertrack → New inquiry → Submit → Print from Archive → Staple Bureau to Registration and desk.

5. Customer Complaints – Get Name and Number → Seat Customer in selected area → Give to GM → Start Ticket in CRM (if complaint is received outside the store).

6. Registration Forms – Fill out Contact Info → Fill out Trade Section → Fill out Vehicle Desired Section → Monthly Payment and Down Payment Goals → Credit Section → Sign Form if Financing.

7. Credit App – Separate App for Each Person. → Fill out App → (income box) How much per hour and number of hours per week → Previous Job if under 2 years at current one.

8. Rebate Sheets – log in to Manufacture site → Generate Vincent report → verify if person

qualifies for extra rebates → Search for Personalized Certificates → Print and Desk Deal.

9. Delivery – Prep vehicle for delivery (wash, vac, clean windows, rear sticker) → Review Owner's Manual → Print Maintenance Schedule → Add Business Cards (sales, service) → Service Walk.

10. Service Walks – Show were to park & enter → Explain the Always $19.95 Oil Change → Explain Service Loaners and Pick up and Drop Off Service → Introduce to writers and Service Manager.

11. Service Loaners – During Hours: Walk customer to Parts Department. After Hours: Copy DL and Ins Card → Fill out Rental Form (Vin & Miles) → Customer Sign → Manager to finalize.

12. Test Drives – Complete Registration form → Copy of DL and Insurance Card → Desk Deal. Zero unapproved test-drives.

13. Budget Customers - Attempt using cash as down payment and financing → Verify Total Funds (Plus TTL?) → Review Inspection Sheet with items noted but not fixed → Inspection by their mechanic → Price as-is and price with issues repaired.

14. Unrealistic Customers – Salt their mouth (showing vehicle) → submit deal → Bring water (present options).

Payment Matrix – Budget Vehicles

Rate	3%		5%		10%		20%	
Term	24	36	24	36	24	36	24	36
$2,500	113	76	115	79	119	85	134	98
$3,500	158	107	162	109	169	119	187	137
$4,500	204	138	208	139	219	149	239	176
$5,500	249	168	254	169	267	187	295	215
$6,500	294	199	299	205	316	219	349	354

Late Model Vehicles

Rate	3%		5%		10%		20%	
Term	60	72	60	72	60	72	60	72
$10,000	189	159	199	169	225	199	279	249
$12,500	236	199	249	109	279	249	349	315
$15,000	284	239	299	249	339	289	419	379
$17,500	329	279	349	299	389	339	475	339
$20,000	379	319	399	339	449	389	559	499
$25,000	469	399	499	419	559	488	699	629
$30,000	569	479	599	509	669	589	839	759

All payments calculated using zero cash down and 5.5% Sales tax.

Mistake Logbook

Date	Name	Unit	Mistake Made	Cost

Trim Level Cheat Sheet

	Ford	*GM*	*Dodge*	*Toyota*	*Honda*	*Mazda*
Cars	S	L	SXT	L	LX	SPORT
	SE	LS	R/T	LE	EX	TOUR
	SEL	LT	SRT	SE	EX-L	GT
	SPO	LTZ		XLE		
	RT					
SUV	BAS	L	SXT	LE	LX	SPORT
	E	LS	R/T	SE	EX	TOUR
	XLT	LT	GT	XLE	EX-L	GT
	SPT	LTZ		LIM		
	LIM					
VAN			SE	L	LX	
			SXT	LE	EX	
			GT	SE	EX-L	
				XLE		
				LIM		
TRUCK	XL	W/T	SLT	SR	RT	
	XLT	LS	LAR	SR5	SPORT	
	FX4	LT	BIG	LIM	RT-L	
	LAR	LTZ	LIM	PLAT